W9-AWN-919

Nothing for
the Nation

NOTHING FOR THE NATION

WHO GOT WHAT OUT OF IRAQ

by

John Hostettler

Although the author and publisher have made every effort to ensure the accuracy and completeness of information contained in this book, we assume no responsibility for errors, inaccuracies, omissions, or any inconsistency herein. Any slights of people, places or organizations are unintentional.
First printing 2008

ISBN 978-0-9800588-0-2
Library of Congress Control Number: 2008920960

ATTENTION CORPORATIONS, UNIVERSITIES, COLLEGES, AND PROFESSIONAL ORGANIZATIONS: Quantity discounts are available on bulk purchases of this book for educational, gift purposes, or as premiums for increasing magazine subscriptions or renewals. Special books or book excerpts can also be created to fit specific needs. For information, please contact Publius House, P.O. Box 5566, Evansville, IN 47716-5566.

To Mom and Dad
Until the roll is called up yonder

Progress, far from consisting in change, depends on retentiveness ... when experience is not retained, as among savages, infancy is perpetual. Those who cannot remember the past are condemned to repeat it ... This is the condition of children and barbarians, in whom instinct has learned nothing from experience.

—George Santayana, *The Life of Reason*

CONTENTS

PREFACE

THE Iraq conflict is the most important public policy issue in the United States today. The U.S. military is embroiled in an ongoing clash with insurgents after toppling the regime of Saddam Hussein. While the struggle to leave Iraq a safer country continues, a question that is crucial to the future of the security and credibility of the United States continues to be asked. Why did the United States invade a country that posed no significant threat to our republic?

The short answer is that the intelligence provided to the president and the Congress of the United States supported the accusation that a program of weapons of mass destruction (WMD) existed in Iraq and, additionally, implied there was reason to believe Saddam Hussein was going to supply these weapons to a terrorist organization third party that would strike his most hated enemy—the United States. However, the intelligence did not support such a claim. As a member of the United States House of Representatives, I stated as much in a speech on the floor of the chamber of that august body on October 8, 2002—two days before the House voted to give President George W. Bush authority to invade Iraq (hereafter referred to as "Iraq Resolution") at his discretion. But if the intelligence supplied to Congress did not support the pronounced justification for our military invasion of Iraq, was it possible to learn the true motivation for those in the administration who would push for such an invasion? Was there other "intelligence" that could be acquired and would inform us of the real reason for a desire for regime change in Iraq? There was.

I have never been employed by any agency of our intelligence community. However, as a result of my twelve years as a member of the House of Representatives Armed Services Committee, I have had the opportunity to glean some appreciation for the work of that critical component of our national security infrastructure. One thing I learned was that very rarely does an interview between a James Bond-type secret agent and the highest leader of a governmental or terrorist organization yield the discovery of the exact motivation and means as to why things happen. Acquiring useful intelligence has much more to do with discerning signs, recognizing patterns, and understanding human nature than does emulation of an Ian Fleming-like scenario. Were there signs and patterns which, when coupled with our understanding of human nature, enlighten us on the actual justification to topple Saddam Hussein? There were. This book is my analysis of and determination made from that intelligence. Understanding the true motivation for our invasion of Iraq based on available intelligence is important. Even more important is our learning sooner rather than later what truly drove the United States to battle.

Recently, an acquaintance who considers herself a conservative told me that the national conversation concerning why we went to Iraq has been exhausted. A conservative colleague of hers offered the idea that people are more concerned with winning the war against the terrorist insurgents who have moved to Iraq since the demise of the Hussein regime. These are unique perspectives from individuals who usually condemn government overreach. Such condemnations from conservatives have been harshest when our military has been deployed for causes not relevant to our national security.

Not long after learning of my acquaintances' views on the current conflict in Iraq, I was viewing C-SPAN's coverage of a conference held in Washington, D.C. The conference was conducted by a conservative foundation and included a throng of conservative icons, reminding the college student attendees of the virtues of conservative values and giving them hope for the future. This latter task was a tall order. The unpopularity of the Republican president and the recent loss of control of Congress to the Democrats made any encouraging subject matter difficult to find.

The attendees asked many questions of the numerous guest speakers and panelists during the course of the conference. Later in this book, I give the account of one question asked of a longtime conservative journalist. The main objective of the question was to learn from the experienced political observer his perspective on the invasion of Iraq. Paraphrasing, the student asked, "Why was there a push for an invasion?" The young man's inquiry convinced me that while it may be a question many conservatives—including my two acquaintances—believe is moot, that viewpoint is not held by most Americans. My acquaintances' opinion of the matter was definitely not consistent with my own regarding this most important foreign-policy predicament of the twenty-first century.

As one of six Republicans in the United States House of Representatives (the House) who voted against the October 2002 resolution to allow the president to invade Iraq, I believe the Iraq invasion is a precedent that conservatives, specifically, and Americans, in general, will come to regret one day. Given the probability of a progressive Democrat victory in the race for the White House in 2008, that day is likely closer than we think. The reason for the likelihood is progressivism by definition finds new justification for government action of all sorts. Why would we think the exercise of military action is immune from this evolutionary approach to public policy? It follows that what conservatives, specifically, and even Americans in general may consider is not a proper justification of expenditure of blood and treasure tomorrow may be entirely in keeping with the next cause *de jour* for the future President Clinton or President Obama or President Edwards, etc. Any conservative opposition to a progressive commander-in-chief's military foray will undoubtedly be answered with quotations uttered during the build up to and execution of the Iraq conflict. These quotations would be supplied from the floor speeches of prominent Republican congressmen and senators or similarly related passages from the transcripts of conservative radio-talk-show hosts.

Therefore, it is incumbent upon conservatives to acknowledge that the conflict in Iraq, which began with the invasion of March 2003, was inconsistent with longstanding principles of the foreign policy of our constitutional republic. I contended as much when I voted against the House resolution that granted President Bush the unconstitutional authority to declare war. I was convinced of it when I learned the true motivation of those who were most invested in selling the case for a "preemptive" strike against the regime of Saddam Hussein.

Nothing for the Nation: Who Got What Out of Iraq is my effort at that acknowledgment. I hope it is not the last such pronouncement from those who claim their public life has been dedicated to the practical application of time-tested principles of American conservatism. Those principles have served us well. If we are willing to return to them by first admitting the violation of those principles by an administration many claim as one of our own, the United States of America will be the better for it.

INTRODUCTION

I T is evident the conservative movement is in disarray following the takeover of the United States House of Representatives by Speaker Nancy Pelosi and other progressives. However, it would be fatal to American conservatism for conservatives to believe the foreign-policy failure in Iraq did not contribute mightily to that takeover. Unfortunately, the airwaves and bookshelves are full of popular conservative voices suggesting the Iraq conflict is a "conservative" foreign-policy success. They may not be saying those words exactly, but when they defend our presence in Iraq, their credibility alone as standard bearers for the conservative movement suggests as much to both conservatives and progressives alike.

Likewise, those in the politically mushy middle, diplomatically referred to as "independents," are similarly impressed with the notion an unjustified war is a conservative triumph. When conservative radio personality "X" or conservative author "Y" defends George W. Bush's decision to involve the United States in the current conflict in Iraq, independents conclude there must be some conservative principle that is characteristic of our activity there. This conclusion is reinforced by independents' knowledge of the fact that the vast majority of Republican House members and senators in 2002 voted to empower the executive branch with this authority. However, the founders of our republic would refute the claim that our invasion of Iraq is even remotely supported by conservative philosophy.

I was one of only three conservatives in Congress to vote against the October 2002 resolution to authorize President George W. Bush to invade Iraq. I did so not in spite of conservative principles but because of them. The proposal violated well-established principles of a conservative foreign policy. These principles have been handed down to us by the likes of Augustine, Thomas Aquinas, and our nation's founders.

First, the Iraq Resolution violated the concept of proper authority. When the framers of the United States Constitution decided to improve on the

Articles of Confederation, they left the authority to take the nation to war "effectually confided to the federal councils"[1] (i.e., Congress) according to James Madison writing in Federalist Paper No. 41. They maintained in the Constitution that "Congress shall have power to … declare war … [and] to make rules for the government and regulation of the land and naval forces."[2] Additionally, in the Constitution, the framers empowered the president only to act as "commander in chief of the army and navy."[3] They did this enlightened by millennia of human history and observing the propensity of a ruler vested with total power to drag their nation into war. These founders also understood that merely writing it on paper did not guarantee that future generations would realize the danger of bestowing so much power in the hands of one person. Maryland delegate to the Constitutional Convention, Dr. James McHenry, provided the account of a lady confronting Benjamin Franklin on the last day of the convention. She inquired of the senior statesman, "Well, Doctor, what have we got—a Republic or a Monarchy?" Franklin replied, "A Republic, if you can keep it."[4] By delegating the decision to attack Iraq to the executive branch, the Congress effectively transformed the republic to a monarchy when it conveyed the most important governmental authority to President Bush.

After the approval of the Constitution by the delegates in Philadelphia, three prominent American citizens, Alexander Hamilton, John Jay, and James Madison, wrote periodic messages to the people of the state of New York in order to convince them ratification of the Constitution was worthy of their support as well as that of their state's ratification convention. There were many issues discussed in scores of what were, essentially, opinion editorials published in newspapers throughout New York. In these opinion editorials—known today as the Federalist Papers—the issue of national defense was considered the most prominent rationale for union under a new Constitution.

Writing in Federalist Paper No. 3, John Jay noted, "Among the many objects to which a wise and free people find it necessary to direct their attention, that of providing for their safety seems to be the first."[5] Citing the instances in which citizens have justifiably endeavored to defend their interests and their persons, Jay continued, "The just causes of war for the most part arise either from violations of treaties, or from direct violence."[6] Having operated in political circles, I can appreciate Jay's use of the phrase "for the most part." This convenient use of what are commonly referred to today as "wiggle words" was meant to provide for the likelihood there may have been in the past an instance when a war was waged and may at some time in the future be an instance when a war may be waged justifiably for some reason other than the two given. This proviso, however, was not meant in any way by Jay to suggest "just" war is waged as a result of instances, including broken treaties, "direct violence" against one nation by another, and whatever other reason a leader may dream up as a "just" cause.

This leads me to the second object of my opposition to the Iraq Resolution—the violation of the principle of proportional response. It was clear Iraq had not engaged in "direct violence" against the United States and had not violated any treaty with us. The case that was made for war demanded we respond to the imminent threat of Saddam Hussein's use of weapons of mass destruction against the United States directly or through a terrorist agent. However, the intelligence available to Congress did not support the allegation of the presence of a WMD program in that country. A vote to allow the U.S. military to invade Iraq gave support to a response that was by no means proportional to the threat. I stated this on the floor of the United States House of Representatives two days before I voted against the Iraq Resolution. Afterward, I wrestled with the fundamental question, "Why are we doing this?" for more than four years.

The question would be answered, generally, by a voice from the past. Returning to the Federalist Papers, John Jay observed the historical inclination of national leaders to drag their countrymen into fruitless and bloody conflict and wrote in Federalist Paper No. 4, "Monarchs will often make war when their nations are to get nothing by it, but for purposes and objects merely personal, such as … revenge for personal affronts; or private compacts to aggrandize or support … partizans."[7]

Before I left office in January 2007, I was satisfied I had learned the true justification, specifically, for our military intervention in Iraq. I am not suggesting that I have an extrasensory perception that revealed the motivation of those who led America into this conflict. Nor did I interview the key players responsible for the push to attack Iraq. The public record, along with information I received in my capacity as congressman, supplied me with sufficient insight regarding their perspective on Saddam Hussein. I was able to compare these personal perspectives with the true nature of the threat posed by Iraq to our national security.

I doubt John Jay considered himself clairvoyant. It goes without saying he did not have the opportunity to interview the individuals so important in the successful marketing of the advantages the United States would gain by starting a war with Iraq. He could not have understood what their sentiments were toward Saddam Hussein's regime. But once again, I am satisfied Jay's words penned more than two hundred years before the invasion of Iraq in March 2003 echoed in the events before and since that time.

I believe John Jay was prescient because he supplied us with the template for the motives and actions of those who led our nation to war in 2003. That template is the basis of the evidence offered in the pages of this book. It is evidence that is immensely more compelling as the justification for our military involvement in Iraq than was the case for a WMD program directed by Saddam Hussein. As a conservative who voted against authorizing the leader of my party to "preemptively" strike Iraq, I am endowed with the calm assurance that Jay's almost prophetic warning reminds us, as in Ecclesiastes 1:9, there is no new thing under the sun.

When you conclude your examination of the case made here, you may question my reasoning, at least, or be passionately incredulous at worst. I can understand why that gambit of responses may arise from conservatives, progressives, and independents alike. That is the beauty of America. Our country is great enough that a clear majority of people can be just as wrong today as they were in October 2002 when they insisted their duly elected members of Congress delegate authority to President George W. Bush to initiate offensive military operations against the people of Iraq. Abraham Lincoln went so far as to say not only can most of the people be wrong more than once but that "*all* the people" allow themselves to be "fool [ed] ... some of the time"[8] (emphasis added). But I ask you, isn't the future of America's children worth the effort to begin to get it right? As a conservative, I mean "right" in every sense of the word.

This book sounds the warning a clear majority of Americans in October 2002 should have heard in the wisdom of John Jay and the other founders. Because whether it's the next Iraq or the next Somalia or the next Vietnam, for that matter, our posterity will be the ones who either benefit from our centuries of wisdom or suffer as a result of our most recent spate of ignorance.

CHAPTER 1

LOYALTY WITH NO BOUNDS

AFTER leaving office in 1993, former president George H. W. Bush was invited to Kuwait to be honored and thanked for the important role he played in liberating that country from Iraq's military in 1991. The United States played the leadership role in the military victory over Saddam Hussein's forces. As the U.S. commander in chief, President Bush masterfully allowed his commanders in the field to use every tool in their arsenal—intellectual as well as physical—to overwhelmingly expel the Iraqi forces from Kuwait. Coalition forces—predominately U.S.—pushed the Iraqi army across the desert to the capital city of Baghdad where, under the advisement of prominent U.S. military leaders, Commander in Chief Bush stopped short of toppling the governing regime.[1] The coalition—most responsibly, the United States—had not "broken" the government of Iraq, and so we did not "own" it. As such, President George H. W. Bush did not involve the American military and taxpayer in the rebuilding of Iraq.

At the celebration in Kuwait, the former president was accompanied by family members, including his wife, Barbara. While at the time it seemed to most of the world the events went smoothly, a plot to murder the former president while he was in Kuwait was uncovered. The U.S. government determined that the Iraqi Intelligence Service (IIS) directed a group of would-be assassins to make their way into Kuwait and kill the one person most responsible for the humiliating defeat of Iraq's military in 1991. It was concluded that such an operation with such a prominent target for assassination could not have been carried out without the consent of—if not initiation by—Saddam Hussein.[2]

The Bush family—father George H. W., mother Barbara, sons and daughters, their spouses, and George and Barbara's grandchildren—is an admirably close-knit one. When the family is together, it is easy to see the love and pride they feel for each other. That feeling of love and pride manifests itself in other noble characteristics, one of which is duty. Eight years after Saddam Hussein most probably consented to the murder of George H. W. Bush, the son of that very well-known target for assassination became commander in chief of the last remaining superpower military on the face of the earth. Revenge is a powerful motivator. On inauguration day in 2001, motive married opportunity.

According to Federalist Paper writer John Jay, it would not be the first time in history that "revenge for [a] personal affront"[3] would have compelled a leader of a mighty military nation to right a great wrong. To a dutiful son, there is only one "affront" greater than a failed assassination attempt of a prominent patriarch: a successful one.

Additionally, Jay observed, in the past, heads of state joined with "partizans"[4] to "aggrandize or support"[5] them in the accomplishment of their goals. What more righteous desire can these partisans act upon than ensuring the security of a divinely appointed homeland for their posterity?

Conveniently, both of these noble aspirations would be fulfilled with the demise of a mutual nemesis.

It has been said most ineloquently that what goes around, comes around. Whatever the motivation—the belief in the presence of a WMD program, duty to family, or a motivation completely foreign to the national security of the United States—the simple reality was what had gone around in 1993 in Kuwait and afterward in places like Gaza was beginning to come around not long after a newly elected president was inaugurated in 2001.

CHAPTER 2

GROWING OPPOSITION TO "NATION BUILDING"

TODAY there is much discussion of both the justification for the United States initiating a military conflict with Iraq and the continuation of a mission to leave that nation better than we found it. After toppling the regime of Saddam Hussein, President George W. Bush found himself continually being asked to justify not only his commencement of violence in Iraq but his retreat on a campaign promise. In 2000, presidential candidate George W. Bush pledged to not engage the U.S. military in nation building. It was a pledge many of us read on his lips.

While I will mostly focus on the justification for "preemption" in Iraq, I also want to spend some time on the political issue of "nation building." Nation building is exactly what began in Iraq after the capture, conviction, and execution of the governing regime that was in power prior to our introduction of ground forces there. To refresh your memory of the political landscape surrounding the issue of nation building prior to George W. Bush's first inauguration, I want to review the principled disagreement with that policy as declared by the Republican Party, generally, and presidential candidate Bush, specifically. Recalling George W. Bush's clearly pronounced opposition to the use of U.S. military force for significant humanitarian purposes will clarify our thinking so we may focus on the actual motivation that drove him and his subordinates in the Pentagon to desire military conflict in Iraq. This is a case where it is almost as important to know what the reasons for our involvement in Iraq were *not* as it is to learn what the reasons for our going there were.

The genesis of the current debate over nation building predated the midterm elections of 1994 and was prominent not only in that election cycle but in the presidential race of 2000. Let me digress briefly into recent history to set the stage in remembering George W. Bush's statements concerning nation building during the presidential campaign of 2000.

Upon entering office in 1993, President Bill Clinton was faced with a foreign-policy dilemma in the Horn of Africa. His predecessor, George H. W. Bush, had begun the process of providing military protection for the humanitarian supply of food to the war-torn country of Somalia. The fall of the socialist government of Mohamed Siad Barre left a governing vacuum that was being filled by warlords who were competing for the right to control portions of the country. Mogadishu, the capital and chief port city, was the prize that elicited the heaviest attention by the strongest warlords and, therefore, experienced the greatest concentration of the fighting.[1] George H. W. Bush had restricted the operation of the U.S. military in Mogadishu to protection of the supplies at the port so that their delivery to Somali and non-Somali relief organizations would proceed relatively unmolested.[2]

President Clinton soon sought a way to expand the use of military force beyond protection of the shipments of food at the point of transfer to the relief organizations. He would attempt the mission of regime change. This meant the United States would attempt to forcibly remove the warlords from their positions of power and put in place a democratic government more sympathetic to the needs of the Somali people. The ensuing tactical debacle in Mogadishu led to the needless deaths of several soldiers and became the inspiration of the book *Black Hawk Down* written by Mark Bowden.[3] Two years after the tragic events depicted in the book and following the departure of U.S. combat forces and UN peacekeepers, the most famous target of U.S. combat operations—the warlord Mohamed Farrah Aidid—declared himself president of Somalia.[4] The failed policy of nation building in Somalia cost the United States precious blood and less valued international prestige.

The lesson of the catastrophe of Mogadishu would be short lived. Later, in Bosnia, President Bill Clinton announced the United States would escalate military operations in the Balkans. This would be an attempt to stabilize a situation that had arisen because the demise of the Soviet Empire had caused ripple effects in the satellite nation of Yugoslavia.

But unlike Somalia, which began with U.S. ground forces providing protection for delivery of food at the ports, the United States had not inserted ground troops in a conflict in the Balkans at the outset of our activity there. This conflict was essentially an ethnic civil war. It was a civil war the rest of Europe had not felt a need to enter. For the United States, it was a foreign civil war that was coming at a time when we were making significant changes to our military capabilities. The nation-building crusade the Clinton administration was to embark upon in Bosnia would take place when the military had undergone three rounds of Base Realignment and Closure (BRAC) and was in the throes of a fourth.

Each round of BRAC is a congressionally mandated reduction in U.S. military infrastructure. Created near the end of the Cold War, BRAC is intended to eliminate surplus military installations made redundant by shifting geopolitical realities and the evolving military requirements that follow. Those changing requirements that result in reduced numbers of facilities invariably lead to lower troop levels to be supported by a smaller infrastructure. The United States had on three occasions since 1988 reduced its ability to carry on military operations by reducing its supporting bases and other installations. All of this occurred during a time when the operational tempo of our fighting forces had drastically increased. This escalation of activity resulted from Operations Desert Shield and Desert Storm and expanding roles in Somalia and the Balkans.

In February 1993, Bill Clinton approached the United Nations to seek permission to airlift humanitarian aid to the embattled region of Bosnia-Herzegovina. He received the nod from Secretary General Boutros Boutros-Ghali and ordered the Pentagon to begin the deliveries, thereby, putting the U.S. military's foot in the door.[5] As the reports of ethnic cleansing piled up, President Clinton's resolve to affect events heightened his desire to utilize military force. Once again, the neighbors of the former Yugoslavia did not feel compelled to introduce significant numbers of their own military personnel in Bosnia at this time. Reluctance on the part of neighbors of the former Yugoslavia to enter the fight led many of us to ask the question, "What is the threat to U.S. national security if Europe is standing on the sideline?" Put another way, "What vital national interest is served by putting America's sons and daughters in harm's way while Europe is neutral to the plight of one of its own?"

This lack of proper justification for U.S. military intervention in the Balkans became a significant political issue in the 1994 midterm congressional campaigns. The issue mix of everything from socialized medicine to "assault weapons" made for a unique political tapestry in 1994. Included in the mix was a foreign-policy debate that centered on the U.S. military as the world's "police force." The outcome of that national debate played a key role in the transition of power in the House of Representatives from Democrat control to Republican control for the first time since the early 1950s.

After complete control of Congress ceded to Republicans in January 1995, the debate over justification for military intervention in the Balkans led to many actions on the part of the 104th Congress. The focal point of attention in the House was President Clinton's inclination to introduce U.S. ground forces into Bosnia. But unlike the situation in 1993 when President Clinton expanded the military mission in Somalia to include regime change, the House of Representatives was no longer controlled by the president's party. It was under the leadership of newly elected Speaker of the House Newt Gingrich and the Republicans.

With the new majority in place in the House of Representatives, there was consideration of several bills and resolutions that expressed significant if not always a majority opinion that U.S. ground forces should be introduced only after Congress authorized and funded such a move. In October 1995, the House passed a resolution that stated as follows:

> No United States Armed forces should be deployed on the ground in ...
> Bosnia ... until the Congress has approved such a deployment.[6]

In November of that year, a bill to prohibit funds for a Bosnian deployment received bipartisan support and stated as follows:

> None of the funds appropriated ... to the Department of Defense may
> be ... expended for the deployment on the ground of United States
> Armed Forces in ... Bosnia ... unless funds for such deployment have
> been specifically appropriated by a law enacted after ... this Act.[7]

The following month, the House passed another resolution at a time when President Clinton was in the process of defying Congress—including many in his own party—by deploying tens of thousands of ground forces to Bosnia. The resolution restated the pronouncements of the earlier resolution as well as the earlier bill and concluded by saying this:

> The House of Representatives … reiterates serious concerns and opposition to the President's policy that results in the deployment of 20,000 members of the United States Armed Forces on the ground in … Bosnia.[8]

It is important to note that this last resolution in December 1995 received the support of sixty-five Democrats who joined 221 Republicans. It is just as important to observe although it is customary for the Speaker of the House to abstain from voting, Speaker Newt Gingrich joined 220 members of his party to send a strong message to the Democrat White House that unjustified deployment of U.S. ground troops was not only an important policy issue but that it would also be an important political issue.

Beyond the political concerns surrounding the introduction of ground forces in Europe to engage in someone else's fight, there was deliberation taking place in the Pentagon. According to his autobiography, *My American Journey,* chairman of the Joint Chiefs of Staff, General Colin Powell, voiced his opposition to the use of ground forces in Bosnia.[9] But the opposition from the uniformed services like that of Congress was to no avail.

In December 1995, Commander in Chief Bill Clinton ordered ground troops to Bosnia to reinforce the Dayton Peace Accords. President Clinton vowed the deployment would be concluded in one year. As was the case for much of what President William Jefferson Clinton said during his tenure as commander in chief, this would be inaccurate. The deployment ended in late 2004.[10] In December of that year, the European Union took over peacekeeping operations from NATO. In the end, Europe took over a mission in which they were more than willing to allow the United States to expend its own military and economic resources in the early, turbulent stages.

As I mentioned earlier, Somalia and Bosnia became issues in the presidential election in 2000. These and other scenarios brought about the further discussion of nation building. The question was asked in a variety of ways but could essentially be stated in this fashion, "For what purpose shall the U.S. military—especially, U.S. ground forces—be deployed?" The U.S.

military—and especially U.S. ground forces—should only be deployed in the defense of the nation's vital interests. As conservatives, this precept is why we believe it is known as the "Department of Defense." While the tragic events that unfolded in places like Somalia and Bosnia were of tremendous concern and possibly deserved diplomatic attention, they did not rise to the level of an ongoing or even imminent threat to our national security. Additionally, if someday the definition of "U.S. vital interests" would be changed to include genocide, despotism, or oppression in some distant land, where in the world would we be able to objectively withhold the use of U.S. ground forces? For conservatives, this question is answered easily and eloquently by John Quincy Adams.

John Quincy Adams was the sixth president of the United States. He was the son of John Adams, second president of the United States. As John Adams's secretary, John Quincy Adams accompanied his father to Paris in 1783 as part of a delegation involved with the signing of The Treaty of Paris. The Treaty of Paris formally ended the War of Independence between Great Britain and the newly formed United States of America. This delegation was merely a continuation of what would become John Quincy Adams's long and illustrious career of public service. His position on the use of U.S. military forces as an instrument of foreign policy is the basis of the conservative perspective. During a speech at a Fourth of July celebration in Washington, D.C., in 1821, Adams elaborated on his position when he stated

> Wherever the standard of freedom and independence has been or shall be unfurled, there will her [America's] heart, her benedictions and her prayers be. But she goes not abroad in search of monsters to destroy. She is the well-wisher to the freedom and independence of all. She is the champion and vindicator only of her own.[11]

These were powerful words in a speech by a prominent government official. This presentation no doubt stirred the thoughts of those who heard it and were taking part in the celebration of the birth of the nation. Adams' personal perspective not only made for good speech material, it would be the foundation of the most prominent statement of foreign policy for the young republic.

Less than two years later, the administration of President James Monroe would be faced with the increasing frequency of actions by European nations in the affairs of the Western Hemisphere. In response to this emerging threat to U.S. influence, Monroe delivered an address to Congress on December 2, 1823, outlining his concerns and warning Europe not to interfere in America's backyard. In a pronouncement that has been dubbed "The Monroe Doctrine," President Monroe was noticeably inspired by the point of view of his secretary of state, John Quincy Adams. It has even been suggested that "The Monroe Doctrine" would be more appropriately labeled "The Adams Doctrine." By declaring his intention to withhold America's military action in the affairs on the other side of the Atlantic, Monroe nearly echoed Adams's Fourth of July speech in 1821:

> Of events in that quarter of the globe [Europe], with which we have so much intercourse and from which we derive our origin, we have always been anxious and interested spectators. The citizens of the United States cherish sentiments the most friendly in favor of the liberty and happiness of their fellowmen on that side of the Atlantic. In the wars of the European powers in matters relating to themselves we have never taken any part, nor does it comport with our policy so to do. It is only when our rights are invaded or seriously menaced that we resent injuries or make preparation for our defense.[12]

Whether the name of the "monster" was Aidid, Milosevic, or Saddam Hussein, it is clear they were monsters abroad whose subjects deserved the warmest regards of our "heart ... benedictions and ... prayers"[13] in the form of the most "cherish[ed] sentiments the most friendly in favor of the liberty and happiness of [our] fellowmen."[14] However, none of these monsters were a threat to the "freedom and independence"[15] enjoyed by citizens of the United States of America. Therefore it was not necessary for America's sons and daughters to play the role of "champion and vindicator"[16] when "our rights"[17] had not been "invaded or seriously menaced."[18]

John Quincy Adams and James Monroe stated then what conservatives believe today. George W. Bush believed it at one time, as well.

CHAPTER 3

CANDIDATE BUSH AND NATION BUILDING

THE use of military force was a topic of discussion in each of the three presidential debates held in 2000. The issue was brought up in some form or another by a moderator or an audience participant. In each forum, Texas governor George W. Bush attempted to distinguish his views on the justification of the use of military force from those of Vice President Al Gore. Because the vice president was obviously not the commander in chief and, therefore, did not have the authority to deploy troops anywhere, Governor Bush alluded to the use of military force by then Commander in Chief Bill Clinton.

Transcripts of each of the three debates have been preserved by the Commission on Presidential Debates and are referenced here. Somalia was brought up only once in all three debates. In the second debate, in Winston-Salem, North Carolina, the discussion of nation building was facilitated by Jim Lehrer of PBS's *NewsHour*. In that debate, Lehrer asked Governor Bush about Somalia and the use of combat forces in that theater of operation. He voiced his opposition to the expanded role of the military when he stated:

> [U.S. military operations in Somalia] started off as a humanitarian mission
> and it changed into a nation-building mission, and that's where the mission
> went wrong … I don't think our troops ought to be used for what's called
> nation-building.[1]

Unlike Somalia, Bosnia received attention in all three debates. The continued presence of U.S. military personnel there made the Balkans a more timely issue. In the first debate, in Boston, Lehrer posed the following question to both Vice President Gore and Governor Bush: "How would you go about as president deciding when it was in the national interest to use U.S. force, generally?" Governor Bush replied:

> I don't think we can be all things to all people in the world ... He [Vice President Gore] believes in nation building ... I believe the role of the military is to fight and win war ... I believe we're overextended in too many places.[2]

After Bush's answer, Lehrer gave an opportunity to Vice President Gore to respond. Gore said:

> I think that there are situations like in Bosnia ... where there's a genocide, where our national security is at stake there.[3]

At this point, Bush invoked the names of two individuals who were prominent in the administration of his father and in the success of Operation Desert Storm in 1991—retired Chairman of the Joint Chiefs of Staff Colin Powell, and retired Commander in Chief U.S. Central Command, General H. Norman Schwarzkopf. The mention of Colin Powell's name was especially important in that it was Powell who had been so forceful as chairman of the Joint Chiefs in his opposition to President Clinton's use of the U.S. military for combat operations in Bosnia.

Bush followed Gore's response by saying:

> I was honored to be flanked by Colin Powell and General Norman Schwarzkopf recently stood by me [sic] side and agreed with me ... If we don't stop extending our troops all around the world and nation building missions, then we're going to have a serious problem coming down the road, and I'm going to prevent that.[4]

In the second debate, Vice President Gore attempted to draw the governor out as to the criteria Bush would use as president to justify the initiation of ground combat operations. The vice president referred to the situation that had evolved in Bosnia, specifically, and asked:

> In some of the discussions we've had about when it's appropriate for the U.S. to use force around the world, at times the standards that you've laid down have given me the impression that if it's something like a genocide taking place or what they called ethnic cleansing in Bosnia, that that alone would not be … the kind of situation that would cause you to think that the U.S. ought to get involved with troops … Now, have I got that wrong?[5]

Bush this time directed his reply back to a discussion of Serbian leader Slobodan Milosevic. Governor Bush had agreed with President Clinton's use of air strikes to help NATO remove Milosevic from power in Serbia. For whatever reason, Bush did not feel compelled to answer Gore's question directly or in the affirmative. This nonresponse by Bush indicated to me that he felt there would be no one left to defend the United States if we sent ground forces everywhere human suffering was taking place. And this perception was made clearer later when the moderator asked Governor Bush to reiterate the point he had made in the first debate regarding nation building. The moderator asked:

> You said in the Boston debate, Governor, on this issue of nation building, that the United States military is overextended now. Where is it overextended? Where are there U.S. military that you would bring home if you become president?[6]

Bush answered in part:

> One of the problems we have in the military is we're in a lot of places around the world … I would very much like to get our troops out of there … I think it ought to be one of our priorities to work with our European friends to convince them to put troops on the ground [in Bosnia].[7]

In the third debate, in St. Louis, the format included questions from audience members recognized by the moderator. One audience member asked the candidates:

> Today our military forces are stretched thinner and doing more than they have ever done before during peacetime. I would like to know ... what you as president would do to ... more selectively choos[e] the time and place that our forces will be used around the world.[8]

Candidate Bush replied after candidate Gore had delivered his answer. It seems the governor may have felt the vice president's answer strayed somewhat from the intent of the questioner when Bush said:

> Your question was deployment ... I'm concerned that we're overdeployed around the world.[9]

It was clear in the record that was established by the forums sponsored by the Commission on Presidential Debates that Governor George W. Bush, candidate for president of the United States in 2000, was not in favor of using military force for the purpose of rescuing some other nation's citizenry from violent oppression, much less that of installing a democratic regime afterward.

Whether he knew it or not, candidate Bush was upholding a tenet of a conservative American foreign policy enunciated by John Quincy Adams, embedded in the Monroe Doctrine, and mentioned earlier in this book. In essence, George W. Bush made it very clear that if elected president of the United States, he was not going to be using the military as the world's police force by sending ground forces "abroad in search of monsters to destroy."[10]

Therefore, I may proceed in the discussion of military operations in Iraq knowing candidate George W. Bush never desired to go there to deliver a ruthlessly oppressed people. In other words, we now know what was *not* a reason for our involvement in Iraq. Now I may discuss the reasons for our going there. We must find other justifications for President George W. Bush's decision to invade a nation whose ability to carry on significant military operations was decimated by the coalition led by his father in 1991.

Many who support the president's decision to preemptively strike Iraq say, "Of course there was another justification. The justification was the intelligence that pointed to a program of weapons of mass destruction." As a member of the United States House of Representatives in 2001 and 2002 and, therefore, keenly interested in the subject of intelligence that pointed to a WMD program, I am able to shed some light on that topic from a unique perspective. Additionally, there is the assertion today that America was led to believe Saddam Hussein and Osama Bin Laden may have been in the process of conspiring to use weapons of mass destruction against the United States. I will touch on that allegation, as well.

CHAPTER 4

9/11: A FALSE PRELUDE

IN George W. Bush's first year as president, I was invited to the Pentagon for a late summer breakfast in the office of Defense Secretary Donald Rumsfeld. About a dozen or so of my colleagues had received the same invitation and we discussed legislation authorizing the Defense Department's programs for fiscal year 2002. It was much later in the calendar year than we had normally considered such annual legislation in the House. But with a new administration from a new party—the party of the congressional majority—and a new secretary of defense, the schedule had slipped significantly. There were differences between the White House's approach in providing for our national defense and that of the House. Conversely, there were portions of the House legislation of which the secretary was especially supportive. It was a pleasant breakfast meeting with good food and cordial dialogue. This mutually respectful approach would be necessary in order to begin the process of moving the first defense-authorization bill for the Bush administration through the House the next day—September 12, 2001. Shortly before 9:00 AM, a uniformed military assistant to the secretary entered the room and politely reminded him he had another meeting scheduled for which he needed to prepare. Secretary Rumsfeld apologized for having to cut the discussion short and thanked us for joining him and talking about the important piece of legislation we would be considering.

As is the case in all such meetings, good-byes are extended periods of time. A few of us left early and made our way out of the secretary's office, down the stairs and out of the massive, five-sided building, and into the parking lot. We had been driven to breakfast from Capitol Hill by Pentagon staff and were awaiting our transportation back to the Hill. As we were waiting on that beautiful September morning, one of my colleagues from Florida, John Mica, received a call from his office on his cell phone. He took the call from a staff member, who informed him the news stations were following a report of a helicopter or small plane that had just crashed into one of the World Trade Center towers.

In September 2001, Representative Mica was the Chairman of the Subcommittee on Aviation for the House Committee on Transportation and Infrastructure. During the August recess just a month earlier, he had held a subcommittee field hearing in New York City at the Port Authority offices in one of the towers. The caller informed Representative Mica that his staff was viewing the plumes of smoke rising out of the tower that had just been "accidentally" struck. He continued to listen to the caller and relayed to us the news reports from his staff.

A few moments after giving us the initial message, a troubled look came across Congressman Mica's face. He then said, with the phone still at his ear, "A second plane has just hit the second tower." He ended the call, and we all concluded this was no accident and that something was terribly wrong. Our driver showed up shortly after the phone call ended. We piled into the minivan and headed for our offices. Approximately thirteen minutes after we left the Pentagon on September 11, 2001, hijacked American Airlines Flight 77 slammed into that building, killing 184 people less than six hundred yards from where my colleagues and I had been standing. What would later become known as the "global war on terror" had commenced.

It did not take much time for al Qaeda to claim credit for the atrocities of September 11, 2001. The leader of the terrorist organization, Osama Bin Laden, became public enemy number one. Soon, the Congress met to authorize the president to hunt down the planners of that heinous operation along with anyone who had given them aid and comfort in their plotting of it. On September 14, 2001, the House of Representatives passed HJRes 64 and the Senate passed SJRes 23, both of which authorized the president

> to use all necessary and appropriate force against those *nations,* organizations, or persons *he determines* planned, authorized, committed, or *aided the terrorist attacks* that occurred on September 11, 2001, or harbored such organizations or persons, *in order to prevent any further* ["future" in

SJRes 23] *acts of international terrorism against the United States* by such *nations, organizations or persons*[1] (emphasis added).

The House resolution passed with but one dissenting vote; in the Senate, support for their resolution was unanimous.

Support for America's defense against terrorism was solid at home. There was similar international support. A coalition soon was created to destroy the organization most closely affiliated with the al Qaeda terrorist network—the Taliban in Afghanistan. Participation in the campaign against the Taliban ranged from significant personnel and matériel support from our usual European allies, such as the United Kingdom, to the first coalition hospital in Kabul supplied and manned by Russia. There was even aerial refueling support from NATO member and predominately Muslim Turkey.[2]

Two months later, a joint session of Congress convened to receive an address from the commander in chief not long after the terrorists flew those airplanes into buildings in New York City and Arlington, Virginia, and into a cornfield in northern Pennsylvania. In attacks that resulted in a greater loss of life than that inflicted by imperial Japan on U.S. forces at Pearl Harbor on December 7, 1941, nineteen hijackers evoked a response from the last remaining superpower military. That response was now the focus of the world. To me, a "backbencher"—a term given to less senior members of the House—the events of the time seemed to transform the chamber of the House of Representatives not only into a different place but to a different time.

I have many times seen the film clips and more often heard the sound clips of President Franklin Delano Roosevelt's speech to Congress following the attacks of December 1941. I never imagined in my wildest dreams I would someday be seated in that same chamber while listening to the president of the United States of America address the nation after having voted to send troops into harm's way following a "dastardly attack" on our country.

On January 29, 2002, President George W. Bush delivered his first State of the Union address to the Congress and the people of the United States. As a member of the House of Representatives, I had endured six such presentations before, delivered by President William Jefferson Clinton. They had always been much longer than they should have been. I was pleased to learn from various sources that George W. Bush was known as a man of relatively few words. (In Washington-speak, forty minutes is, by definition, "few words.") It was most assuredly shorter than any of President Clinton's speeches. However, this was not going to be the standard State of the Union presentation. U.S. combat forces were in harm's way because on September 11, 2001, foreign agents murdered thousands of Americans on U.S. soil.

I believed the foreign-policy portion of the 2002 State of the Union address would be similar to the speech in November 2001. And while the weight of that portion of the president's speech centered on September 11, 2001, and ongoing military operations in Afghanistan, he began beating the war drums for another front in the global war on terror.

In a presentation that has been dubbed the "Axis of Evil" speech,[3] President Bush called out three nations whose support of terror organizations was well documented by numerous nations' intelligence services. In an effort to be "steadfast and patient and persistent in the pursuit of two great objectives," President Bush said the second such objective was "to prevent regimes that sponsor terror from threatening America or our friends and allies with weapons of mass destruction." In disclosing the "true nature" of the governing regime of North Korea, President Bush said it was "a regime arming with missiles and weapons of mass destruction, while starving its citizens." He said the government of Iran "aggressively pursues these weapons [of mass destruction] and exports terror, while an unelected few repress the Iranian people's hope for freedom."[4] And he had the most to say of the third nation in the triad. Of Saddam Hussein's regime, President Bush stated:

> Iraq continues to flaunt its hostility toward America and to support terror. The Iraqi regime has plotted to develop anthrax, and nerve gas, and nuclear weapons for over a decade. This is a regime that has already used poison gas to murder thousands of its own citizens—leaving the bodies of mothers huddled over their dead children. This is a regime that agreed to international inspections—then kicked out the inspectors. This is a regime that has something to hide from the civilized world.[5]

He concluded his discussion of the three despotic governments by saying:

States like these, and their terrorist allies, constitute an axis of evil, arming to threaten the peace of the world. By seeking weapons of mass destruction, these regimes pose a grave and growing danger. They could provide these arms to terrorists, giving them the means to match their hatred. They could attack our allies or attempt to blackmail the United States. In any of these cases, the price of indifference would be catastrophic ... All nations should know: America will do what is necessary to ensure our nation's security ... I will not wait on events, while dangers gather. I will not stand by, as peril draws closer and closer. The United States of America will not permit the world's most dangerous regimes to threaten us with the world's most destructive weapons.[6]

As I pondered President Bush's remarks, I thought it was clever for him to have used the term "evil" to describe a set of regimes whose ideology was so divergent from that of the United States. Another president once used the same term to explain another regime that had cast its shadow of oppression over much of the world. When Ronald Reagan described the Soviet Union as the "evil empire," weak-kneed simpletons everywhere decried his comments as belligerent and naïve. But he was right. History has proven that his resolve freed hundreds of millions of souls from the fear of that great tyranny. Though I considered it clever for Bush to borrow from The Gipper, I likewise felt it was a departure from the true concern.

I felt that the major imperatives were finding Osama Bin Laden and destroying al Qaeda. North Korea, Iran, and Iraq were concerns that predated the current administration and would probably last through the end of the same. But the allegation of a WMD program in Iraq would be an issue that gained traction both for the White House and in Congress. And this preoccupation with Iraq confused me on two fronts.

The first source of confusion was, as I just mentioned, a desire to draw attention away from the real objective of resolving the 9/11 issue. Osama Bin Laden and al Qaeda were the most important military targets. The second source of confusion was the fact our military was already engaged in Iraq.

After the virtual obliteration of the Iraqi military in Operation Desert Storm, the coalition left the country. With the remaining war-making capabilities Saddam Hussein possessed, he turned his wrath upon the Shia-dominated south of Iraq. This was an act of vengeance for the part the

south played in facilitating coalition forces in their march to Baghdad during
Desert Storm. Likewise, in northern Iraq, the United States continued to
be concerned with the ongoing tensions between the governing regime in
Baghdad and the ethnic minority Kurdish population in that area. In an effort
to protect the northern and southern areas of Iraq from Saddam, the United
States set up no-fly zones with Operation Northern Watch and Operation
Southern Watch, respectively. These operations consisted of thousands of
military aircraft sorties over the areas to discourage Saddam from carrying
out reprisals against Iraqis in these areas. While these aerial military activities
were not 100 percent effective in protecting every Shiite in the south[7] and
every Kurd in the north,[8] their justification was more related to a policy of
"containment" of the Iraqi leader.

The Bush administration spoke of this containment policy on several
occasions. For example, in a State Department briefing held in late July 2001,
a question was asked concerning an episode involving a U.S. warplane that was
patrolling the skies over southern Iraq. After the State Department spokesman,
Phillip Reeker, referred the question to the Pentagon, he reiterated U.S. policy
by stating:

> He [Saddam Hussein] remains a menace and that is why our policy has
> been focused on keeping him isolated, containing the threat that he has
> posed to his neighbors, to the region, to regional stability, and continues
> to pose. And that is why we have made Iraq policy a priority. We continue
> to review aspects of that, we continue to work at the United Nations in
> terms of the sanctions policy.[9]

In late July 2001, the U.S. military was extensively involved in "containing
the threat ... to regional stability"[10] that Iraq posed. With the ongoing military
actions of Operation Northern Watch and Operation Southern Watch, not
only was the region's stability enhanced, Saddam's threat to his own people
was similarly contained.

However, by late January 2002, the world learned that the United States
had grown weary of containment. President George W. Bush's first State of
the Union address of January 29, 2002, signaled a new direction in our dealing
with the regime in Baghdad. The question I had, though, was, "Why was it
necessary to take a new direction in policy toward Iraq when Saddam was

'contained' and the whereabouts of Osama Bin Laden were unknown?" You can understand my initial confusion. The answer later became clear. Saddam no longer had to be contained. After the 9/11 attacks and with the proper message, Saddam was a monster who could now be destroyed.

CHAPTER 5

IRAQ: THE HARD SELL THAT WASN'T

WHILE the president and others in his administration turned their attention from al Qaeda and honed their message on Saddam's WMD, Congress began focusing on Iraq as well. As a member of the House Armed Services Committee, I attended hearings and briefings in both classified and open settings where the focus was the allegation of a WMD program in Iraq. As the dialogue between members of the House and the administration progressed, I became more and more anxious about the direction we were obviously heading. Initially, I tried to recall if weapons inspectors had ever reported a large cache of biological or chemical weapons being uncovered and then left undestroyed when the inspectors were ejected from Iraq in 1998. No such report had been made.

Before I go any further, I want to define some terms. One of the most important aspects of any discussion of weapons of mass destruction is the description of the items in question. Are these items, in fact, weapons? There is a significant difference between the individual components of a weapons system and an actual weapon. Components of various subsystems that may be manipulated and later combined with other subsystems to make up a complete weapon are not necessarily weapons in themselves. An example is the distinction between a satellite-delivery system and a ballistic-missile system. A large rocket is necessary to overcome the gravitational force of the earth and push a satellite into space. Likewise, a large rocket is necessary to push an intercontinental ballistic missile thousands of miles to its intended target. The presence of an advanced industry dedicated to the production of large rockets does not necessarily reveal the presence of a ballistic-missile program. It may, in fact, signal the presence of an aggressive satellite-production capability to serve the communications, information, or entertainment industries of the country in question or the world.

Biological or chemical agents are often referred to as "precursors." Without these precursors as components, there can be no biological or chemical weapon. However, the presence of these precursors alone does not constitute a program of weapons of mass destruction. For example, any nation that has any substantial agriculture industry that includes the manufacture of inputs, such as, insecticides, has a program of producing chemical-weapons precursors. Any country that has a life-sciences industry very likely maintains the infrastructure for, at least, a potential program of creating biological-weapons precursors. But, once again, the presence of biological or chemical precursors does not, in and of itself, indicate a WMD program. Given that many countries have some or all of these capabilities, we would be very busy indeed if we allowed the potential threat posed by all of these precursor-producing nations to be the basis of military preemption and acted accordingly.

You will recall the numerous allegations of Saddam Hussein using chemical weapons against his own citizens. The horrific photographs that chronicled the murderous cruelty that was the basis of these accounts made indelible marks on our psyches. But the picture that soon came to everyone's mind when they considered the potential use of WMD against the United States was best characterized by National Security Advisor Condoleezza Rice. Less than a year after the world observed the images of those two towering infernos in New York City, she suggested a much more threatening specter in a September 2002 CNN interview with Wolf Blitzer.

Mr. Blitzer asked Dr. Rice about her understanding of Iraq's nuclear weapons capabilities. Her response was as follows:

> "We know that he [Saddam Hussein] has the infrastructure, nuclear scientists to make a nuclear weapon ... And we know that when the inspectors assessed this after the Gulf War, he was far, far closer to a crude nuclear device than anybody thought—maybe six months from a crude nuclear device ... The problem here is that there will always be

some uncertainty about how quickly he can acquire nuclear weapons. But we don't want the smoking gun to be a mushroom cloud."[1]

The idea of a nuclear weapon being detonated over a major metropolitan area of the United States gave rise to an understandable urgency in the country and in Congress.

I remember being invited to the West Wing of the White House not long before the House voted on the resolution to authorize force against Iraq. The invitation was for a meeting with Dr. Rice, CIA Director George Tenet, and CIA Deputy Director John McLaughlin, along with a dozen or so of my House colleagues. The purpose of the meeting was to allow House members to hear from the CIA leadership and the national security advisor and to ask questions in order to help us in our deliberation on the preemptive use of military force against Iraq. A highlight of the meeting occurred when an aluminum tube was revealed and presented for our examination. At the time, a set of these aluminum tubes was the topic of much debate surrounding the presence of a WMD program in Iraq. At this White House meeting, as well as elsewhere, it was suggested that these tubes were manufactured to be components of a centrifuge that would be used to process fissile nuclear material. This refined nuclear material could then be used in a radiological or nuclear weapon.

As an aside, even though I am a mechanical engineer, I have never worked in the nuclear-energy industry except for an abbreviated period of time shortly after graduating from college. I was employed by a contractor at a nuclear-power-plant construction site. During my stint at the site, I never witnessed anything approaching the sophistication of a fissile-material centrifuge. So to show me an aluminum tube in hopes I would be convinced of the presence of a nuclear centrifuge in Iraq was a bit of a reach. Observing my colleagues handling and studying this tube with their years of law school and political-science education to inform them of its intent was no less intriguing to me.

But most interesting to me at this meeting was the definitive approach by the leadership of the CIA in their depiction of this set of tubes. At the same time, there were reports these tubes were not intended for components of a nuclear centrifuge. Along with the centrifuge theory, it was suggested by some in the intelligence community that the aluminum tubes were actually intended to be used as components of a Multiple Launch Rocket System

(MLRS). An MLRS is, generally speaking, a conventional weapons system made of numerous tubes, each containing a conventional rocket with a high-explosive warhead. While the rockets in an MLRS can be fitted with a biological or chemical warhead, the weapon system itself is usually considered a conventional one. The inconsistency in the portrayal of the aluminum tubes was not helping me conclude a nuclear WMD program existed in Iraq. Although the aluminum tube controversy was not creating a mushroom-cloud picture in my mind, it was helping to form a cloud of confusion for me in this run-up to the vote to preemptively strike Iraq.

Another concern I had after hearing numerous reports of the presence of a WMD program in Iraq was the source of the intelligence that was being relied upon. It seemed we were getting much of our information from Iraqi dissidents. Iraqi expatriates whom we believed had special insight into the current situation in Iraq were telling us what they believed we wanted to hear about a WMD program there.

Remember, I said these dissidents were telling us what "we wanted to hear." The most notable of these dissidents was a gentleman by the name of Ahmed Chalabi. Chalabi was the leader of an organization of Iraqi exiles referred to as the Iraqi National Congress (INC). The INC was funded by U.S. tax dollars as an outside opposition group many believed would play a key role in Iraq after the demise of Saddam Hussein. This demise, it was believed initially, would take place from within. This was obviously not happening nearly quickly enough in the opinion of some, Chalabi prominently included.

As the number of hearings and briefings I attended grew, my list of questions narrowed significantly. One question I always asked was, "Where are you getting this information?" In many cases, the answer included some allusion to Iraqi exiles. In many cases, these Iraqi exiles included Ahmed Chalabi. My follow-up question was always, "What are *our* people telling us?" Almost invariably, the answer was akin to, "We do not have human intelligence resources (i.e., spies) in country (Iraq) or elsewhere capable of acquiring the requisite intelligence on their programs." This consistent line of response continued to elicit a question I would pose to members of my staff, namely, "Why are we basing so much of our understanding of Saddam's programs on the word of someone (Chalabi) who seems to have so much to gain by our removing the current governing regime in Iraq?" I concluded Chalabi and the numerous other dissidents would tell us whatever they thought would be necessary to compel us to remove Saddam from power.

The follow-up to my internal question about where we were getting our intelligence was a question regarding sources we were not depending upon for important information. This follow-up question was, "Why are we basing so little of our decision to preemptively strike a foreign nation on the information we are obtaining from our own intelligence assets?" Along with human intelligence sources, the United States' intelligence community has substantial technological capabilities. I was continually amazed at the lack of support for the allegation of a WMD program in Iraq from these assets, as well.

While the inconsistencies in the intelligence (e.g., aluminum tubes) and the suspect nature of the sources of much of the information on Saddam's WMD program (e.g., dissidents) concerned me, there was an additional issue I would raise at every opportunity. The question I asked at numerous classified briefings was very simply, "Where are the weapons of mass destruction?" If we were going to war based on the presence of a program of weapons of mass destruction, there were good reasons we should have known the location of these weapons.

First, the presence of WMD was the justification for sending America's sons and daughters into harm's way. After all, if we were going to initiate war with another country, should we not have had some idea of the location of the source of the justification of our invasion? At the time, I used a hypothetical scenario as an analogy to make my point to staff, friends, and family. It was possibly not the best analogy, but it was the best I could do under the circumstances. It was a car analogy. At the risk of unintentionally invoking the cinematic classic, *Dude, Where's My Car,* here it goes.

Suppose it is a Friday evening. After a long week of work—or school, depending on your audience—you and a friend wish to have a relaxing night out. Your friend offers, "Hey! Let's take my car."

This sounds like a good idea to you, and you innocently ask, "Great! Where is it?"

Imagine your surprise when your friend confidently answers your inquiry with, "I have not a clue."

After you finish chortling as a result of what you thought was a good joke, you see the emotionless look on your friend's face, and you repeat, "No, seriously, where is your car?"

Your friend's response is as redundant as it is perplexing, "No, seriously, I don't have any idea where it is."

Not wishing to imperil your relationship with your longtime compatriot, you begin a line of seemingly logical questioning with, "Is it in your driveway?"

He responds, "I don't know."

You continue, "Is it in your garage?"

"I don't know."

"Did you leave it at work/school?"

"I can't say."

"Did you leave it at the scene of an accident?"

"I am not sure."

"Did you fail to pick it up from the dealer after you purchased it?"

"I can't recall."

After a while, would you not begin to doubt your friend had a car with which to transport the two of you? I know I would. But that's just me. And it was I who believed if we didn't know where these weapons of potentially horrific effect were, should we not have waited until we knew where they were—if they were there at all?

It was this idea of their potentially horrific effect that led to a second important reason for knowing where the WMD were actually located in Iraq. Any military operation resulting in the removal of the governing regime in Iraq would require a large number of ground forces to accomplish the mission. Those ground forces would undoubtedly face a significant challenge to their intended goal. The goal would be regime change. The tyrannical head of that regime would throw everything he could at the invading forces to not only challenge them but to thwart them in the accomplishment of their goal.

It was claimed that Saddam Hussein had weapons of mass destruction at his disposal. It was believed he knew where these weapons were located. There was every reason to believe this tyrant knew what the invading forces of the last remaining military superpower would do in order to remove him from power. Saddam also knew if he was deposed, his last moments on the planet would be spent at the end of a rope or in some other similarly uncomfortable scenario. We may conclude Saddam likely would have used those weapons of mass destruction against those overwhelmingly superior conventional forces in an attempt to forestall that appointment at the end of a rope. Given the likelihood of a tyrant's use of WMD against our volunteers, I believed it would be advantageous to know the whereabouts of these weapons.

After spending much time contemplating the proposition of the preemptive use of military force against Iraq, I knew a few things. This is what I learned about Iraq's WMD program, according to the intelligence that was available to me and 434 of my colleagues in the House of Representatives and to one hundred senators:

1. Iraqi dissidents with much to gain told us a WMD program existed in Iraq.
2. We had virtually no significant, firsthand knowledge from U.S. intelligence assets of such a program.
3. We didn't know where the weapons of mass destruction were in Iraq.
4. There was no significant tie between al Qaeda and Saddam Hussein's governing regime.

I concluded I could not justify support of a preemptive military strike on Iraq based on the intelligence that was available to me.

Some will say, "But, John, you were just a backbencher in the lower house. Could you not have understood that the president is privy to information that is simply not available to you in your subordinate capacity?" This perception of the relationship between Congress and the intelligence community is usually held by Americans belonging to one of two groups. The first group is made up of individuals who watch too much television. You know the standard plot. There is some national crisis. The scene begins with a close-up of the shadowed face of an actor portraying the president of the United States. After the president barks out his first question, the camera pans the inadequately lit room and reveals military uniforms adorned with more metal than runs through a Midwest steel plant in a week. The military officers seated around the large oblong or rectangular table, along with the suit-and-tie leadership of the various intelligence agencies, then provide the commander in chief with the "intel" to which only he may be made aware. The next scene includes the same actor standing behind a properly appointed and presidential-looking podium, announcing to the country his decision based on that undisclosed bit of intelligence no one else may know. In this Hollywood-based understanding of government, the members of Congress each play the situational equivalent of a potted plant.

The second group who hold to the idea that members of the Article I branch of the federal government are, in cases such as the decision to go to war, virtually irrelevant, is made up of Americans who believe the utterances of certain members of the Article I branch of the federal government. Individuals in this second group listen intently to a select group of senators and representatives who today tell their fellow citizens, "If I knew then what I know now, I would have voted differently." As someone who spent no small amount of time in hearings and briefings that focused on the intelligence—or what we "knew then"—I am puzzled by this pronouncement.

My question to these former colleagues is, "What is it you 'know now'?" Do you "know now" of individuals—such as Mr. Chalabi—who fabricated a story about a WMD program in Iraq in order that we might take military action to rid his homeland of a tyrant? If so, to borrow the words of country-music singer George Strait in his song "Ocean Front Property," I have some "ocean front property in Arizona" I would like to sell you. Or is it you "know now" there were no WMD found in Iraq? My question then would be to these regretful legislators, "Are you saying you 'know now' of the absence of weapons of mass destruction? These are the same weapons of mass destruction of which the location we 'knew then' I suppose?" But it was, in fact, the case "then" that not a single person in the administration could tell us where the WMD were located.

There are other members of Congress who steer the distraction in a very different direction by claiming, "I was lied to." These members of the House or the Senate would have us believe the intelligence community in meeting its obligation to Congress did not withhold a nugget of truth that was passed on to the president according to that Hollywood version I mentioned earlier. These legislators would have you believe agents in the intelligence community actually told them something *in addition* to the truth. This *additional* bit of "intelligence" was, as the story is told today, a "lie" that convinced, say, a junior senator from the great state of New York to vote to authorize the president to unilaterally order a preemptive military invasion of another country.

The actual truth is this: Congress created every single intelligence agency in the federal government. Congress funds every single intelligence agency in the federal government. Every employee of every intelligence agency knows these two things. Additionally, every employee of every intelligence agency—as well as their commander in chief—knows two additional things: Congress may eliminate any or all intelligence agencies in the federal government. Short of that, Congress may eliminate any or all programs (i.e., jobs) in any intelligence agency in the federal government.

Therefore, you may conclude the following: although the intelligence community is fully aware that members of Congress cannot possibly know everything about day-to-day intelligence operations, it does realize that every speck of intelligence made available to every federal legislator had better be, once again, the truth, the whole truth, and *nothing but the truth*. This is especially the case when it comes to a decision to put America's sons and daughters—and with them, our way of life—into harm's way.

I would be remiss, however, if I did not mention another class of legislator. This group was made up of Republican colleagues who were troubled by the lack of substantiation between the claim of a WMD program in Iraq and the intelligence offered as the evidence of such a program. These colleagues ultimately put their trust in the leader of their party. That trust was bolstered by a hope that the GOP commander in chief would never subject our men and women in uniform to unjustified danger. This trust was misplaced. We know that now. My former colleagues know it now. And I am saddened by the betrayal they have endured.

CHAPTER 6

A NEW ADMINISTRATION AND AN OLD NEMESIS

THE intelligence community did not lie to me. I did not believe the intelligence supported the case for the presence of a WMD program in Iraq. Given that, I wanted to know what was compelling the administration to push such a weak case. In other words, what was the Bush administration's justification for wanting to invade Iraq? Why did President George W. Bush, himself, want to remove Saddam Hussein from power? Or if it were not President Bush's desire to remove Saddam, who in his administration was pushing such a feeble rationale for war? Did someone else in the Bush administration desire the demise of Saddam as a result of an even higher calling than the national security of the United States? If they did, were they in a critical position to actually effect that demise?

After I had determined that the intelligence did not support the case for a WMD program in Iraq, I turned my attention to the possibility that President George W. Bush was motivated to remove Saddam Hussein from power for reasons other than national security. That Saddam Hussein's national intelligence service conspired to assassinate former president George H. W. Bush while he was visiting Kuwait in 1993 was a fact established by U.S. intelligence sources. The assassination attempt drew a military response from then President Bill Clinton when he ordered cruise missile attacks on the Iraqi Intelligence Service (IIS). It was a weak reaction from a weak commander in chief. The response was faint especially in the sense it targeted those who were, more than likely, merely carrying out orders. No one believed the IIS would have targeted such a prominent world citizen without the imprimatur of the Iraqi head of state. Put another way, we can only imagine what would have awaited the subordinate of Saddam Hussein who would have unilaterally implemented a plan that had raised the ire of the one nation most responsible for Iraq's crushing defeat on the field of battle just two years prior. No, Saddam knew about the plan. If he did not actually order it himself, he at least knew about it and gave it his blessing. A military strike of the IIS in 1993 probably reinforced all of Saddam's notions about the new commander in chief as well as America's lack of resolve to reenter the fray. But in January 2001, a new sheriff came to town. It was a new sheriff with a good memory—especially when it came to his family.

There had to be a reason—apart from national security—that this administration believed Iraq was the member of the "axis of evil" that should be dealt with first. I have already mentioned the ongoing military operations maintaining no-fly zones in the skies over Iraq and the virtual annihilation of Saddam's conventional war machine during Desert Storm. There were significant issues with the other members of the "evil" triad that made them, in comparison to Iraq, much more of a potential threat.

Iran, for example, was no friend to the United States. They had in their possession fissile nuclear material that we had provided to a previous government there. Their collaboration with the North Koreans had resulted in the indigenous production of an intermediate-range ballistic missile—the Shahab. Speaking of the third member of the "axis," North Korea had an ongoing nuclear program and was not only well known for its proliferation of ballistic-missile technology but had produced a multistage, long-range ballistic missile. The U.S. intelligence community was not fully aware of the capability of this long-range missile until it flew over northern Japan in 1998.

Therefore, we had not only strayed from the primary objective of destroying al Qaeda, but we had also focused on the one regime of the three mentioned in the president's 2002 State of the Union address least able to inflict damage on us or our interests abroad.

I suspected the son of the target of the failed 1993 assassination attempt along with some in his administration still held a grievance against the Iraqi leader. Feeding my suspicion was the subject matter of some of their public remarks. For example, in a speech at the annual convention of the Veterans of Foreign Wars in August 2002, Vice President Dick Cheney chronicled the disconcerting record of Saddam Hussein's leadership. In moving through the litany of abuses, Cheney said America was, "after all, dealing with the same dictator … who dispatched a team of assassins to murder former President Bush as he traveled abroad."[1] You will recall that Cheney served as secretary of defense under President George H. W. Bush during Operation Desert Storm. While similar remarks were in other speeches delivered by the vice president, the use of the name "Bush" subsequently was dropped.

At a National Republican Congressional Committee gala held in Washington, D.C., Cheney once again ran through a list of grievances against Saddam Hussein. The event was held just eight days prior to the vote by the House of Representatives that authorized the president to strike Iraq. This time, his mention of the attempt on the life of the father of the current president was more generic. He said, "The Iraqi regime has attempted to assassinate the Emir of Kuwait and a former President of the United States."[2]

And it was President George W. Bush himself who made a very personal reference to the events of April 1993. The reference came at a gathering at which he no doubt felt comfortable in letting his guard down and showing his deepest feelings on the matter. At a late September 2002 fundraiser for U.S. Senate candidate John Cornyn in Houston, Texas, President Bush described Saddam Hussein by saying, "After all, this is a guy that tried to kill my dad at one time."[3]

Though I could not justify a preemptive strike against Iraq to eliminate a WMD program that probably did not exist, I sought to learn if the United States could justify such a strike based on a rationale supported by the intelligence record. This search led me to a briefing given by Secretary of Defense Donald Rumsfeld prior to the House vote on the Iraq Resolution. I asked the secretary if it were possible to obtain the support of some nations for military operations against Iraq if we based our case on the fact we knew Saddam tried to murder former president George H. W. Bush. This support could include our traditional European allies who were not yet supportive of a preemptive show of force. I believed former heads of state should not be held open to the possibility of assassination for actions taken when they held their high office. Surely, the leaders of France, Germany, and possibly even Russia could agree with us that in the family of civilized nations, this principle could be defended even with military force. A common objection to political assassination would possibly elicit favorable support from foreign governments. After all, a recent example of such an attempt was supported

by the intelligence record. Because there was credible information that
pointed to the assassination attempt in Kuwait, removing a regime bent on
politically motivated murder was potentially a more plausible justification for
international military conflict than the less than convincing assertion Iraq
maintained a WMD program.

As I recall the response from Secretary Rumsfeld, what struck me most
about it was, for a split second, he looked at me as though I had read his
mind—or, possibly, the mind of someone he was very close to. His response
after that brief moment of silence was profound. He suggested such a
justification may be characterized as something akin to revenge. Secretary
Rumsfeld concluded such a characterization would not be helpful and should
not be used as justification for plunging a nation into war.[4] He convinced me
if not the commander in chief.

At the same hearing, I asked Secretary Rumsfeld a follow-up question
about another issue that, while related to the general topic of revenge,
concerned the expulsion of weapons inspectors from Iraq and that occasion's
link to the nation of Iran. As you recall, after years of attempting to determine
Saddam Hussein's progress at complying with international demands he
destroy all his means of producing WMD, inspectors were thrown out of
Iraq in 1998. And as I mentioned earlier, the eviction of weapons inspectors
did not take place after they had uncovered some clandestine WMD program.
Such a discovery would have revealed Saddam's violation of post–Gulf War
conditions placed on his regime. In fact, the inspectors were almost certain
Iraq had divested itself of weapons of mass destruction. The concern
inspectors and the international community at large voiced at the time of the
inspectors' removal was they had not been able to conclude 100 percent of
Iraq's "reported" stockpiles of WMD had been adequately destroyed.[5] The
issue that did not receive much public discussion at the time was the focus of
my second question to the secretary of defense at the briefing.

I continued in my questioning of Secretary Rumsfeld. As a preface to
my second question, I remarked it would be of more interest to Iran than to
the United States should the world learn Saddam had destroyed his WMD
program. I went on to ask the secretary if Iran became aware their belligerent
neighbor no longer had the weapons it used against Iran in the 1980s war,
what would have stopped Iran from exacting revenge on Iraq? I concluded
my query of the defense secretary by asking, "After we virtually destroyed

Iraq's conventional military capabilities in 1991 and had been, hypothetically speaking, the driving force in the determination of the demise of its WMD threat, would the United States come to Saddam Hussein's aid in a war initiated by Iran?"

The secretary dismissed the idea that disclosure of the absence of WMD in Iraq would have evoked retaliation from Iran.[6] I understand the question may have been a stretch. I find it ironic, however, that there is much discussion of Iran's possible involvement in support of the insurgency in Iraq, which commenced after the fall of Saddam's regime. The likelihood of Iran's support of a militant opposition in Iraq against the United States begs a question. If Iran is willing to support an insurgency in Iraq while there are more than 150,000 U.S. military personnel there, what would Iranian leaders have been willing to do to Iraq after it had been revealed that Saddam had lost most of the war-making capability he had used in the 1980s when he allegedly gassed thousands of Iranian women and children? That question will only be answered after the U.S. military withdraws from Iraq. That will be the time the majority Shia population in Iraq may look to its predominately Shia Persian neighbor for political and cultural direction.

CHAPTER 7

SADDAM AND 9/11: A NONEXISTENT TIE THAT BINDS

IN the justification to strike Iraq following September 11, 2001, I have covered much of the allegation of a presence of a WMD program in Iraq. You will recall that there was also talk in the media of a link between Osama Bin Laden's al Qaeda terrorist organization and the governing regime of Iraq. Speculation was offered by National Security Advisor Condoleezza Rice to CNN's Wolf Blitzer that we could witness a mushroom cloud as the "smoking gun,"[1] confirming the link between Saddam's WMD program and the organization that perpetrated the horrific events of 9/11. For me, this Bin Laden/Hussein connection was the most perplexing aspect of the entire debate surrounding a preemptive strike of Iraq. It was perplexing because any connection between al Qaeda and Iraq similar to the one that was known to exist between al Qaeda and the Taliban would have made Saddam's regime susceptible to a U.S. military strike. That military operation would have been authorized by a law enacted shortly following the attacks of 9/11.

As I mentioned in chapter four, on September 14, 2001, three days after terrorists struck the United States, Congress passed "a joint resolution to authorize the use of United States Armed Forces against those responsible for the recent attacks launched against the United States."[2] The resolution was signed into law by President Bush later that month and authorized a military response to the tragic events of September 11, 2001. The potential targets of that response would be determined by the president and were to include those *nations,* organizations, or persons he determines planned, authorized, committed, or *aided the terrorist attacks that occurred on September 11, 2001, or harbored such organizations or persons,* in order *to prevent* any *further* ["future" in SJRes 23] acts of international *terrorism against the United States by such nations,* organizations or persons[3] (emphasis added).

The entire resolution is located in appendix A. The language was clear. Any nation that played any role, including a supportive one, was subject to attack. The president was clearly authorized—at his discretion—to order such an attack on such a nation. A nation whose activities in support of the actions taken by al Qaeda on 9/11 would have been responsible for "direct violence"[4] against the people of the United States. One of John Jay's two explicit justifications for making war would have been satisfied. A formal congressional declaration of war against that sovereign nation would have, no doubt, followed.

This idea of linkage between the perpetrators of 9/11 and Saddam Hussein was the topic of questions in our briefings as well. The CIA personnel who briefed members of the House would continually remind us that there was "no [significant] linkage"[5] between al Qaeda and the government in Baghdad. Since the invasion of Iraq, there have been many individuals who have claimed the administration "lied" to the American people on this point. This is a false claim for two reasons. First, if the Bush administration believed there was linkage between Saddam Hussein and the events of 9/11, they would never have had to bother with Congress following the September 14th congressional resolution. Second, I don't recall the administration ever saying there was a link between the two.

At this point, I know what you must be saying: "John you must have been asleep during this time because I recall them mentioning a link—constantly!" If I may be so bold, what you heard was not the mention of a "link" but rather a mention of the two entities—al Qaeda and Saddam—in close proximity in remarks delivered by the president, the vice president, and others of the Bush administration prior to congressional votes to authorize force against Iraq. Let me give some examples of remarks made by the Bush administration where there is mention of Saddam and 9/11 but no linkage drawn between the two.

On October 1, 2002, National Security Advisor Condoleezza Rice delivered the annual Wriston Lecture at the Waldorf Astoria Hotel in New York City to a gathering of the Manhattan Institute. In her presentation, she spoke of 9/11 and Saddam Hussein:

> It will take years to understand the long-term effects of September 11th. But there are certain verities that the tragedy brought home to us in the most vivid way.
>
> Perhaps most fundamentally, 9/11 crystallized our vulnerability. It also threw into sharp relief the nature of the threats we face today …
>
> We will break up terror networks, hold to account nations that harbor terrorists, and confront aggressive tyrants holding or seeking nuclear, chemical, and biological weapons that might be passed to terrorist allies. These are different faces of the same evil. Terrorists need a place to plot, train, and organize. Tyrants allied with terrorists can greatly extend the reach of their deadly mischief. Terrorists allied with tyrants can acquire technologies allowing them to murder on an ever more massive scale. Each threat magnifies the danger of the other. And the only path to safety is to effectively confront both terrorists and tyrants.
>
> For these reasons, President Bush is committed to confronting the Iraqi regime, which has defied the just demands of the world for over a decade. We are on notice. The danger from Saddam Hussein's arsenal is far more clear than anything we could have foreseen prior to September 11th.
>
> The Iraqi regime's violation of every condition set forth by the UN Security Council for the 1991 cease-fire fully justifies—legally and morally—the enforcement of those conditions.
>
> It is also true that since 9/11, our Nation is properly focused as never before on preventing attacks against us before they happen.[6]

On August 26, 2002, Vice President Dick Cheney spoke to the annual convention of the Veterans of Foreign Wars in Nashville, Tennessee, about the threat posed by Saddam and the perpetrators of 9/11:

> But the challenges to our country involve more than just tracking down a single person or one small group. Nine-eleven and its aftermath awakened this nation to danger, to the true ambitions of the global terror network, and to the reality that weapons of mass destruction are being sought by determined enemies who would not hesitate to use them against us.

> It is a certainty that the al Qaeda network is pursuing such weapons, and has succeeded in acquiring at least a crude capability to use them. We found evidence of their efforts in the ruins of al Qaeda hideouts in Afghanistan.

> As we face this prospect, old doctrines of security do not apply ... It's a lot tougher to deter enemies who have no country to defend. And containment is not possible when dictators obtain weapons of mass destruction, and are prepared to share them with terrorists who intend to inflict catastrophic casualties on the United States.

> The case of Saddam Hussein, a sworn enemy of our country, requires a candid appraisal of the facts ...

> ... Saddam has perfected the game of cheat and retreat, and is very skilled in the art of denial and deception.

> ... What he wants is time and more time to husband his resources, to invest in his ongoing chemical and biological weapons programs, and to gain possession of nuclear arms ...

> ... We are, after all, dealing with the same dictator ... who has been on the State Department's list of state sponsors of terrorism for the better part of two decades.

In the face of such a threat, we must proceed with care, deliberation, and consultation with our allies. I know our president very well. I've worked beside him as he directed our response to the events of 9/11. I know that he will proceed cautiously and deliberately to consider all possible options to deal with the threat that an Iraq ruled by Saddam Hussein represents.[7]

On September 25, 2002, President Bush addressed Republican senators at their annual National Republican Senatorial Committee dinner in Washington, D. C. He spoke of al Qaeda and Saddam and the need for a response:

Not only will we pursue al Qaeda one person at a time, not only will we resist terror wherever it lurks, we will also deal with madmen who harbor and develop and want to use weapons of mass destruction.

I made a decision to call upon the international community to join us in holding Saddam Hussein to account. I did so at the United Nations because I want the United Nations to be an effective body ... The United Nations must be willing to uphold resolution. The United Nations must be strong enough to hold Saddam Hussein to account.

After all, he's defied the United Nations for 11 years; he's thumbed his nose at the world ... He's a man who has got weapons of mass destruction, yet lies to the world. He's a man—he's a man who needs to be brought to justice.

And the choice is his to make; and the choice is the United Nations' to make. He must destroy his weapons of mass destruction ... And the United Nations must uphold its resolutions. The choice is theirs. But if they choose not to, for the sake of our future, for the sake of our freedom, we will not let the world's worst leader threaten us, blackmail us, or hurt us with the world's worst weapons.[8]

And on October 7, 2002, in Cincinnati, Ohio, three days before the House would vote to authorize him to strike Iraq, President Bush once again reiterated the threats posed by Saddam Hussein and al Qaeda as he believed it:

Tonight I want to take a few minutes to discuss a grave threat to peace, and America's determination to lead the world in confronting that threat.

The threat comes from Iraq. It arises directly from the Iraqi regime's own actions—its history of aggression, and its drive toward an arsenal of terror.

We also must never forget the most vivid events of recent history. On September the 11th, 2001, America felt its vulnerability—even to threats that gather on the other side of the earth. We resolved then, and we are resolved today, to confront every threat, from any source, that could bring sudden terror and suffering to America.

Members of the Congress of both political parties, and members of the United Nations Security Council, agree that Saddam Hussein is a threat to peace and must disarm. We agree that the Iraqi dictator must not be permitted to threaten America and the world with horrible poisons and diseases and gases and atomic weapons ...

... And, of course, sophisticated delivery systems aren't required for a chemical or biological attack; all that might be required are a small container and one terrorist or Iraqi intelligence operative to deliver it.

And that is the source of our urgent concern about Saddam Hussein's links to international terrorist groups.

We know that Iraq and the al Qaeda terrorist network share a common enemy—the United States of America. We know that Iraq and al Qaeda have had high-level contacts that go back a decade. Some al Qaeda leaders who fled Afghanistan went to Iraq. These include one very senior al Qaeda leader who received medical treatment in Baghdad this year, and who has been associated with planning for chemical and biological attacks. We've learned that Iraq has trained al Qaeda members in bomb-making and poisons and deadly gases. And we know that after September the

11th, Saddam Hussein's regime gleefully celebrated the terrorist attacks on America.

Iraq could decide on any given day to provide a biological or chemical weapon to a terrorist group or individual terrorists. Alliance with terrorists could allow the Iraqi regime to attack America without leaving any fingerprints.[9]

In all four of the examples given, you will notice that not one time do any of the speakers suggest Iraq was involved in any way with 9/11. Note the president mentions that Iraq and al Qaeda "share a common enemy—the United States of America."[10] However he stops short of saying they colluded to attack the United States on September 11, 2001. While the president says members of al Qaeda had been trained at some time by Iraqis, he stops short of implying the training was in connection with the actions on 9/11 in the United States. And this is important in that, technically speaking; the terrorist pilots of the hijacked planes received their flight training in the United States and not with the aid of Saddam Hussein.

The president did not say Iraq was tied to the tragic events of September 11, 2001. He did not say it because he knew it was not true. Granted, if he did believe Iraq was connected to the terrorist attacks of 9/11, he would not have had to say it. He also would not have had to lobby his fellow citizens and their elected leaders in the Congress for separate legislation authorizing him to specifically strike Iraq. Such authority already existed as a result of legislation passed shortly after the attacks of 9/11. By his attempts to persuade the country and the Congress to topple Saddam Hussein along with his refusal to exercise authority vested in him by the September 2001 congressional resolution to militarily engage Iraq as a nation that gave assistance in the 9/11 terrorist attacks, President George W. Bush clearly indicated his denial of a link connecting Saddam to 9/11. Once again, it is important to know what was *not* a reason for invading Iraq in March 2003.

The assertion that Saddam Hussein maintained a WMD program in Iraq was the justification presented by the Bush administration to sell a preemptive strike on Iraq. It was the only justification. There was no link between Saddam Hussein and the events of 9/11. If there were any link that was alluded to, it was the potential link between the alleged presence of a WMD program in Iraq and a future alliance with some terrorist organization—al Qaeda or someone else—that was being implied.

Interestingly, leaders in the Bush administration were not the only ones taking this tack. A prominent citizen from the Middle East—former prime minister of Israel Benjamin Netanyahu—was going there, as well. He was the citizen of a country who was all to familiar with terrorists and their destructive ways.

Shortly before the October 10, 2002, vote in the House of Representatives to authorize the president to initiate hostilities against Iraq, members of the House were invited to one more briefing by members of the intelligence community. Representatives from the CIA and the Defense Intelligence Agency (DIA) briefed House members in the Rayburn House office building. The floor was then opened up to members for questions, and I ultimately had my opportunity to make what had become my standard inquiry:

1. Where are the WMD, specifically, in Iraq?
2. Where did we get the intel informing us of the presence of a WMD program in Iraq?
3. What do *our* people know about the presence of a WMD program in Iraq?
4. What is the linkage between the governing regime in Baghdad and al Qaeda?

The answers were the answers I had received for months to basically the same questions, and they were essentially, respectively, as follows:

1. We don't know
2. Iraqi exiles
3. Virtually nothing given the closed nature of Iraqi society to outsiders and lack of information from technological assets
4. None of any consequence

After receiving the answers to my questions, I left the briefing. Accompanying me out the door was a colleague. When we cleared the doorway of the hearing room, he asked me, "John, how are you leaning on this vote to go to war?" I replied I was going to oppose the resolution. His response was, "Last week, I attended a briefing given by Benjamin Netanyahu, and I was ready to lead troops into Baghdad myself. Now, I'm wondering why we are doing this." It was the first time I had heard mention of the former prime minister of Israel briefing members of Congress on this issue. The reference to Mr. Netanyahu brought to my attention another aspect of this whole discussion of a WMD program in Iraq. An incident in recent history had crossed my mind on several occasions prior to my colleague's conversation with me. And it was especially the discussion of a nuclear WMD program that talk of Benjamin Netanyahu brought to mind.

In 1981, as a response to the construction of a nuclear-power generating station in Iraq, Israeli warplanes destroyed the Osirak construction site. This daring military strike was a preemptive action taken by Israel. The action was based on intelligence Israel had received that suggested the electricity-generation use of the nuclear power concealed the true motivation of Saddam Hussein's interest in this unique energy source. The Israelis wanted to make sure Saddam would not be able to acquire the proper fissile material necessary to construct a nuclear weapon he could use against the Jewish state.[11] For me, the question was, "If Israel was willing to unilaterally and preemptively strike Iraq in 1981 over the issue of a possible nuclear WMD program, why was a second such strike from the Israelis not a more recent piece of history?" The answer to that question would come after the vote. And while it would be less complex than most are willing to admit, John Jay warned us of the possibility of its occurrence more than two hundred years ago when he spoke of government leaders who make "private compacts to aggrandize or support … partisans."[12]

Because the president did not believe Saddam was tied to the events of 9/11, it would be necessary to make a compact. But it was not the kind of compact Jay spoke about that would answer the question of why we were going into Iraq. It was a compact to say how we would do it. The question of how we would do it would be answered easily. We would do it together. The people would speak through their elected leaders. There would be votes in the House of Representatives and the Senate. Those votes would reflect the overwhelming popular support for a fight with that monster abroad—Saddam Hussein.

CHAPTER 8

THE VOTE

THE House of Representatives scheduled debate on HJRes 114 entitled "Authorization for Use of Military Force Against Iraq Resolution of 2002." The debate took place October 8–10, 2002. Twenty hours were allotted for consideration of the joint resolution to give all members the opportunity to speak on the issue of granting the president the discretion to topple a foreign government. This is an important point. The resolution was not a declaration of war against a foreign nation. The framers of the Constitution gave that discretionary authority to Congress and Congress alone. Though there have been numerous occasions in U.S. history where the nation has been plunged into military conflict without the use of a formal declaration of war as provided for in Article I, Section 8 of the Constitution, the case before the Congress was one of the United States initiating hostilities against a sovereign nation.

From Thomas Jefferson and the Barbary pirates to George W. Bush and the Taliban, Congress has authorized military action against what have been, essentially, international criminals operating under no national flag. These occasions did not rise to the necessity of a formal declaration of war due to the fact there was not a conflict between two governments as recognized by the community of nations. Article I, Section 8 of the Constitution is clear in its requirement for Congress to assume the leadership role when it comes to the issue of making war against another sovereign nation.

You may wish to debate me on precedents, such as, Korea and Vietnam. I do not intend to enter that debate. The simple fact is I was not alive during the Korean conflict and was thirteen years of age when the United States formally ended significant military operations in Southeast Asia. I did not feel compelled by actions of previous Congresses and previous congressmen in the manner which I would uphold my oath to "support and defend the Constitution of the United States." In October 2002, the House of Representatives was poised to repeat the mistakes of Korea and Vietnam by delegating explicit and exclusive congressional authority, as outlined in the Constitution, to another branch of the federal government. The mechanism to delegate such authority is found nowhere in the Constitution to which members of Congress swear to "bear true faith and allegiance."

It follows that Congress was just as culpable in our nation's foray into Iraq as was the president. That is, Congress was just as responsible as to how we became embroiled in hostilities in Iraq beginning March 2003 as was President Bush. To that extent, this is no more "Bush's War" than it is "Kerry's War," "Edwards's War," "Clinton's War," "Reid's War," "Schumer's War," "Bayh's War," or "Murtha's War." And speaking of significant support for the Iraq conflict by these prominent Democrats, it is a tragic irony that the "peace at all costs" party did not play the role of the party of the loyal opposition as it should have in this case. Ironic in that I have no doubt that if Senate Majority Leader Tom Daschle, then Senate Democrat Whip Harry Reid, Senator Hillary Clinton, Senator and soon-to-be 2004 Democrat presidential nominee John Kerry, et al would have objectively examined the intelligence and disregarded the polls, it's likely Democrat presidential hopefuls would not have to answer so many difficult questions in 2007 and 2008. But that would have taken courage. A political system driven by polls and not by principle has little tolerance for outmoded ideals such as courage. There lies the tragedy. The tragedy is that the courage displayed on the battlefield is not rivaled by the courage of those who desire the title "commander in chief."

The truth is that the overwhelming support in both chambers of Congress merely reflected the magnitude of public support for going into Iraq. In September 2002, a Pew Research Center survey found that 64 percent of Americans favored U.S. military action to remove Saddam Hussein from power.[1] This popular groundswell of support for plunging the nation into conflict may be attributed to President Bush's desire to remove Saddam Hussein from power along with the high job-approval rating his presidency enjoyed at the time. That being said, the intelligence did not support the argument being made that a WMD program in Iraq was ongoing. I believed it at the time and said so during consideration of the Iraq Resolution in the House of Representatives.

On October 8, 2002, I was yielded time to speak for five minutes on the Iraq Resolution. As a member of the House of Representatives, I was not one who would frequently participate in floor debates in the House. However, this time was different. This time, we were considering the placement of U.S. military personnel in harm's way in defense of our vital national interests. This consideration was profound for many reasons.

First, we were initiating military conflict with a sovereign nation. The justification for our potential invasion of Iraq was meeting with significant international skepticism. At the outset, some might say I was nothing short of a "new world order" sycophant of the United Nations or worse—of France. Nothing was further from the truth. My legislative record on such issues as the maintenance of sufficient military capabilities to go it alone when necessary was well documented. Similarly, the record that reflected my disdain for the UN's treatment of the United States was also firmly established. However, from the beginning of the United States, there has been a healthy humility that has adorned our foreign policy, especially when it comes to the issue of military conflict.

In no less an example than the Declaration of Independence—the birth certificate of the United States—and in the words of no less a statesman than Thomas Jefferson, this country has treaded softly when making decisions that would, in all probability, elicit a hostile response. You will recall that in the Declaration of Independence, by "declar[ing] the causes which impel them to the separation" from Great Britain, and speaking for the colonial subjects of His Majesty, Jefferson yielded to "a decent respect to the opinions of mankind." Although he was known as a true Francophile, I am sure had you asked Mr. Jefferson, he would have been able to offer numerous specific examples of those in the family of nations whose opinion he did not have a "decent respect." Once again, I have always believed that the United States should be able to go it alone if necessary. This would be after we had, as a country, exhausted our traditionally exercised "decent respect to the opinions of mankind." It has always seemed to me that the last remaining military superpower is the one entity best equipped to exercise the practice of humility.

A second reason that consideration of the Iraq Resolution was profound was that volunteer war fighters were going to be asked to sacrifice life and limb. If the United States was going to ask this of our men and women in uniform, we had to be sure that the cause was just and real. No "might be" scenario could be considered appropriate justification for sending America's sons and daughters into harm's way. I was just as certain on October 8, 2002, that America's military personnel were going to die and be maimed as I am now that thousands have died and tens of thousands have been maimed in the Iraq conflict. Anything less than a sure thing on the WMD program justification meant a devaluing of the life and limb of my fellow citizen's son or daughter.

And finally, consideration of the Iraq Resolution was profound in a context that some may consider political or even partisan. There is little disagreement that the Republican-controlled House of Representatives was "carrying the water" for the leader of the party on this issue. This would be the case on many other issues during the six years of George W. Bush's presidency in which a Republican majority existed in that chamber. On the other end of the Capitol was a Democrat majority in the Senate. Democrat Majority Leader Tom Daschle was supportive of the Republican White House on the issue of preemption in Iraq. However, you will recall that it was the departure of Senator Jim Jeffords from the Republican Party while serving in 2001 that gave Daschle his title and razor-thin control.

Returning to the House consideration, it would be disingenuous of progressives to suggest this concept of water carrying was exclusively a Republican or conservative phenomenon. Anyone who thinks so need only read the *Congressional Record* at the point immediately prior to my floor speech on the Iraq Resolution. There you will find that a Democrat solicited support for the Iraq Resolution from members of his party by hearkening back to a vote that saw a majority of his party supporting then president Bill Clinton's military intervention in the Balkans. Representative Howard Berman, a Democrat from California, stated:

> I would remind my colleagues in my own party that this body voted on, and 181 of my democratic colleagues supported, the authorization of the use of air strikes to bomb key targets in Yugoslavia in order to stop humanitarian [sic] slaughter of Kosovars without a Security Council

resolution, after the bombing had already started, and thought, properly so, that we were engaging in the right position for the United States.[2]

It was clearly within precedent for members of the commander-in-chief's party to lead the support of his military excursions. However, I had hoped that the Republican Party would be reluctant to exercise military force. I held out this hope because I considered the Republican Party to be the standard bearer for the conservative movement. The GOP would practice conservatism by upholding the framers' intent, especially when it came to making war. Recounting founding father John Jay's comments from Federalist Paper No. 3, war would be waged as a result of "violations of treaties, or from direct violence."[3] Consequently, an America governed by a conservative Republican majority would, therefore, exercise military force on the occasion it was evident to all objective observers that war was the last resort in preserving our way of life. I concluded such would not be the case with the Iraq Resolution, and the prewar intelligence—or lack thereof—was central to my conclusion.

As I mentioned earlier, I was not prone to spending much time speaking on the House floor regarding every issue that arose. This time, however, I decided to take my turn. The members' speeches and the final vote were somewhat anticlimactic. Most of the time prior to the floor speeches and final vote was spent determining if Saddam Hussein was an imminent threat to our national security. After concluding that he was—or, in my case, was not—the floor speeches and the vote on the resolution were mere formalities. They were formalities, procedurally speaking. In another context, they were, historically speaking, profound statements for each respective House member and senator as well as the nation as a whole.

While my speech was not long, it did sum up my thoughts on the question of "preemptively" striking Iraq. The entirety of the speech can be seen in appendix B. Following is the essence:

> Mr. Speaker, … we are not discussing how America should respond to the acts of terrorism on September 11, 2001. That debate and vote was held over a year ago; and our men and women in uniform, led by our Commander-in-Chief and Secretary of Defense, are winning the war on terrorism. It is with their blood, sweat, and tears that they are winning, for

every one of us who will lay our heads down in peace this night, the right to wake up tomorrow, free.

No, Mr. Speaker, the question before us today is, "Will the House of Representatives vote to initiate war on another sovereign nation?" ...

Today, a novel case is being made that the best defense is a good offense. But is this the power that the Framers of the Constitution meant to pass down to their posterity when they sought to secure for us the blessings of liberty? Did they suggest that mothers and fathers would be required by this august body to give up sons and daughters because of the possibility of future aggression? Mr. Speaker, I humbly submit that they did not ...

We are told that Saddam Hussein might have a nuclear weapon; he might use a weapon of mass destruction against the United States or our interests overseas; or he might give such weapons to al Qaeda or another terrorist organization. But based on the best of our intelligence information, none of these things have happened. The evidence supporting what might be is tenuous, at best.

Accordingly, Mr. Speaker, I must conclude that Iraq indeed poses a threat, but it does not pose an imminent threat that justifies a preemptive military strike at this time ...

War should be waged by necessity, and I do not believe that such necessity is at hand at this time. For these reasons, Mr. Speaker, I urge my colleagues to please vote "no" on the resolution to approve force at this time.[4]

On October 10, 2002, the House of Representatives voted overwhelmingly, 296–133, to authorize the president to preemptively strike Iraq at his discretion. I was one of six Republicans who did not support the party's leader in this vote to supply him with the authority for which he had lobbied the Congress and the country. My decision to vote against the resolution was based on the intelligence that was made available to me. Am I saying the intelligence informed me there was not a WMD program in Iraq? No. In this case, even I understood how difficult it would have been, given our limited access to the entire region of Iraq, to prove definitively that Iraq did not have such a program. The vote to authorize the commander in chief to initiate hostilities against a sovereign nation came down to this question, "Did the intelligence made available to the Congress of the United States, adequately inform us that a WMD program is ongoing in Iraq at the time of this vote?" The answer to that question for this member of the United States House of Representatives was "No."

After the Iraq Resolution passed both the House of Representatives and the Senate overwhelmingly, there was a substantive assessment of my vote against the resolution. There was also the question of the electoral fallout resulting from a conservative Republican voting against his party's president. Compounding my dilemma was the nature of the disagreement. The leader of my party desired to initiate hostilities against a foreign nation that had, it was alleged, the resources (i.e., WMD) and motivation (i.e., Operation Desert Storm) to provide terrorists with the means to deliver destruction to the United States. While it is not a small thing to oppose the leader of your political party on any of his initiatives, it is a different thing altogether to oppose him on an issue as popular as striking Iraq was. You may add to that the country's anxiety so soon after 9/11 and the image of a mushroom cloud over a major metropolitan area of the United States, yielding us that "smoking gun" of which National Security Advisor Condoleezza Rice spoke. All of these combined to give us the makings of a rather discontented electorate, generally, and party base, specifically. And it showed. From irate calls to my campaign office from prominent Republicans to one of the closest elections of my career, the Iraq Resolution was one of the single most politically damaging votes I ever cast. It was also the vote I would spend more of my political and post-political careers explaining than any other.

Both before and immediately following the midterm elections of 2002, I found myself in many conversations that centered on my justification for voting "no" on the Iraq Resolution. I would explain I voted against the resolution because I did not believe the intelligence supported the president's assertion that a WMD program existed in Iraq. The question that would sometimes follow that explanation would be, "How could more than two-thirds of the House and three-fourths of the Senate understand the intelligence to tell them just the opposite of what you concluded, John?" At times, this question was sometimes asked in the context of electoral success. The questioner was certain voters would not overlook an incorrect vote on an issue of such importance to our national security. However, more often, it was asked because the questioner believed I had misjudged the intelligence.

The matter of misjudging the intelligence would most often take the form of a more straightforward inquiry and would simply be, "What if you're wrong, John?" My answer was similarly straightforward and was always the same, "I hope I am." I would then be compelled to explain this admission. Why did I hope I was wrong on the most important issue in my political career? If I was correct and there was not ample intelligence to justify a preemptive strike against Iraq, it may be because there was not a WMD program there. If we were not able to uncover a WMD program in Iraq, the United States would have initiated a military conflict with a sovereign nation without just cause. The geopolitical implications of such a blunder that would undoubtedly lead to massive casualties experienced by the offended nation can only be equaled in tragedy by the loss of life and limb of the volunteers in uniform who swore an oath to defend the same Constitution as did members of Congress. I believe now as I believed then that one politician's electoral demise resulting from his incorrect vote on a matter of such profound national security implication pales in comparison to the aforementioned calamities measured in such dreadful carnage.

CHAPTER 9

AMERICA INVADES IRAQ

ON January 28, 2003, President Bush delivered his first State of the Union address following the historic vote by Congress to authorize him to strike Iraq. In that speech he made several claims about the WMD capabilities of Iraq. While some of the allegations such as that of the British government having "learned that Saddam Hussein recently sought significant quantities of uranium from Africa"[1] were accompanied by disclosure of sources, many more were not. I believed that if he was able to disclose the United Kingdom as a source of such profound intelligence, he would have disclosed others if they existed and had been considered credible. I continued to doubt we were headed down the right path. However, it was in this address the president announced that Secretary of State Colin Powell would be delivering a presentation to the United Nations where he would make the case against Saddam Hussein. As I mentioned earlier, I am not a big fan of the UN. Regardless, I was hopeful that Secretary Powell would have the means and opportunity to offer the international body a much more plausible argument against the regime in Baghdad than had been made previously.

To reiterate, at this point, the issue was no longer in the hands of Congress. The Article I branch of the federal government had ceded its authority to the Article II branch. Every one of the 435 members of the House and one hundred senators was now an observer along with our almost three hundred million constituents.

In keeping with the schedule the president had promised in his State of the Union speech, Secretary Powell delivered his presentation to the United Nations' Security Council on February 5, 2003. This would be an opportunity for the United States to make its best case that Saddam Hussein posed an imminent threat not only to our country but to the world, as well. This best case would be made with the best intelligence that the United States could possibly afford to share with the international body.

There would obviously be information that the Bush administration would not be willing to share with the UN because the disclosure of such intelligence would potentially divulge the means by which it was acquired. These revelations would alert nations unfriendly to our vital interests, including Iraq. Future intelligence gathering would be made more difficult by putting our human sources in danger and rendering our technological capabilities less useful. The sensitivity to divulging classified intelligence to an international organization such as the UN is always an issue. No such consideration is allowed when informing members of Congress of classified information.

By virtue of being elected by the people, a member of the House or Senate is endowed with a top-secret clearance. This clearance allows him or her to be privy to our nation's most guarded insights. Therefore, it would be unlikely that Secretary Powell could pass on any significant intelligence concerning the presence of a WMD program in Iraq that had eluded a member of Congress. I had chosen not to lend my support in sending our country down a path to war. On the other hand, I was hopeful that this insightful and deliberative production before the UN would convince me the path down which we were clearly heading was one that was justified by the facts.

As I watched Secretary Powell on TV make the case to the Security Council for the presence of a WMD program in Iraq, it did not take long for my hope to dissipate. Shortly into his presentation, he stated, "The material I will present to you comes from a variety of sources. Some are U.S. sources … Other sources are people who have risked their lives to let the world know what Saddam Hussein is really up to."[2] Once again, we were relying on "sources" that had a vested interest, one way or another, in the removal of Saddam Hussein from power. I was once again hopeful that we would not be basing our decisions on information that was not substantially verified by our own intelligence community. But this was not to be the case. Later, Secretary Powell remarked:

> My colleagues, every statement I make today is backed up by sources, solid sources. These are not assertions. What we're giving you are facts

and conclusions based on solid intelligence. I will cite some examples, and these are from human sources.[3]

These were, indeed, "human" sources. They were human sources with all the fallibilities and desires that come with them. Unlike the human sources Secretary Powell was referring to, employees of the U.S. intelligence community will ultimately lose their jobs if passion or revenge or some motivation other than the cold, hard facts guides their analysis and reporting. The "exiles" or "defectors" or whomever we chose to listen to had nothing to lose and their homeland free of Saddam's oppression to gain by telling us what we wanted to hear. It was about midway into the secretary's presentation that the hope that had begun dissipating early on disappeared altogether.

Secretary Powell presented a depiction of what he claimed were biological-weapons labs that were described to U.S. officials by "an eye witness, an Iraqi chemical engineer" who was "hiding in another country with the certain knowledge that Saddam Hussein will kill him if he finds him." I beheld an artist's rendering of "solid intelligence" supplied to us by an Iraqi "eye witness."[4] When I observed this illustration, which seemed to be so critical in Secretary Powell's presentation, I changed the channel.

It was not out of disrespect for Colin Powell that I moved to other televised programming. In truth, I had for years believed that President George H. W. Bush erred in taking the advice of then Chairman of the Joint Chiefs of Staff Colin Powell, when he did not finish the fight in Iraq and depose Saddam Hussein in 1991. But I came to understand over time that General Powell had been correct. I have concluded that (this is not the "Powell Doctrine," but my own) if we are not willing to remake an entire country, along with its culture, in our own image, we would be better served to merely destroy their ability to make war and be done with it. It was not out of a lack of respect for Secretary Powell that I changed the channel; I simply did not find it necessary to continue to view this particular rerun. At the UN, the Secretary of State asked the world to support the president's desire to send America's sons and daughters into harm's way because an Iraqi had told us about the presence of a WMD program in Iraq even though none of our own intelligence assets could verify this presence. The secretary's offering to the UN resembled presentations I had seen before—often.

In March 2003, the president exercised the war-making authority that Congress had delegated to him and commanded U.S. military forces to invade Iraq. Saddam Hussein might have thought that the commander in chief of the armed forces of the United States might have been convinced to hesitate as a result of significant international opposition to the invasion. Army and Marine Corps units racing across Iraq toward Baghdad, no doubt, dispelled any such uncertainties. By April 2003, it was likely that Saddam knew of his fate if U.S. forces did not repeat the scenario that played out on the outskirts of the capital city during Operation Desert Storm. Given there was another President Bush in command this time, the leader of Iraq may have held out some small hope that the events of 1991 would be replayed. I am sure that even that small hope was dashed when Saddam witnessed the presentation before the UN by the one person—Colin Powell—who many believed was most responsible for saving him from regime change twelve years earlier. There would be no repeat performance.

It seemed Saddam Hussein would have done everything in his power and used every weapon in his arsenal to prevent that second, very different, act from playing out. At least, that is what my militarily inexperienced judgment was. And it was that inexperienced judgment that led me to ask a question of Secretary of Defense Donald Rumsfeld.

My concern that we did not know where the WMD were located in Iraq was heightened during the early stages of the military campaign. After several days of early success by our military, Secretary Rumsfeld addressed a group of House members at a weekly briefing. When he opened his presentation up for questions, I asked, "Secretary Rumsfeld, recalling the early hours and days of Operation Desert Storm, the objective was to substantially degrade the enemy's ability to carry on military operations prior to the insertion of ground forces. The military not only destroyed the command, control, and communications capabilities of the enemy but also destroyed much of the potential war-fighting capabilities so ground forces would have the greatest advantage possible on the battlefield. Why did we not destroy Saddam's weapons of mass destruction early in this campaign given they would have likely been used against our ground forces?"[5] His answer was direct and succinct, "We didn't know where they were."[6]

So there you have it. Not only did we not know where the WMD were prior to Congress' vote to authorize the president to preemptively strike a foreign nation, we did not learn of their location between the vote and Secretary Powell's presentation to the United Nations. We did not obtain a confirmation of their location between the secretary's UN presentation and the initiation of air attacks on Iraq similar to those that initiated Desert Storm. Likewise, we learned an additional zero amount of information about the location of WMD between the time we commenced air strikes and the time we introduced large numbers of ground troops into the conflict.

None of our technologically advanced tools for acquiring information or those "human" sources that Secretary Powell mentioned in his Security Council address could tell us where the most devastating weapons held by Saddam were located. Therefore, we were subjecting our military personnel to an unspeakable uncertainty that was virtually nonexistent in Desert Storm. This uncertainty would not last long.

CHAPTER 10

HUNTING FOR JUSTIFICATION

O
N May 1, 2003, President George W. Bush landed aboard the aircraft carrier USS *Abraham Lincoln* and announced, "Major combat operations in Iraq have ended. In the battle of Iraq, the United States and our allies have prevailed. And now our coalition is engaged in securing and reconstructing that country."[1]

I found it ironic and yet accurate that the commander in chief had referred to the month-and-a-half conflict as a "battle." But what else could he say? To have used the term "war" would have been disingenuous. It is Congress that retains the exclusive and explicit authority to declare war according to Article I, Section 8 of the United States Constitution. The world had viewed the toppling of that immense statue of Saddam Hussein just weeks prior and while the tyrant's location was not yet known to coalition forces, it was merely a matter of time before he would be found and brought to justice. There was probably the same level of certainty that the presence of a program of weapons of mass destruction would soon be revealed. With "major combat operations" concluded, the coalition forces would be virtually unimpeded in their search for the evidence of such a program. The only obstacle to the speedy discovery of that evidence would be the occasional shower of rose petals and demands of parades reminiscent of our own Fourth of July celebrations by euphoric, liberated Iraqis.

But as the hunt for the justification of the "battle of Iraq" progressed, certainty soon turned to reservation. Reservation evolved to doubt. Doubt gave way to realization. And realization ended in astonishment—and excuses.

According to a published account written by Barton Gellman in the *Washington Post* on May 18, 2003, a U.S. military site-survey team entered what

U.S. intelligence had labeled "Possible SSO Facility Al Hayat"[2] about the same time President George W. Bush announced the end of major combat operations in Iraq aboard the USS *Abraham Lincoln.* SSO was the acronym for Saddam Hussein's Special Security Organization. When the team of military personnel chosen for their expertise in various fields of interest regarding WMD reached the inner sanctum of the facility, which was the seventeenth such object of their attention to date, they did not find any weapons of mass destruction. Instead, they uncovered a "cache of vacuum cleaners."[3] This particular search yielded similar results to the previous sixteen. According to the *Post* account, the team had previously "dug up a playground, raided a distillery, seized a research paper from a failing graduate student and laid bare a swimming pool where an underground chemical weapons stash was supposed to be."[4] As I read this story, I couldn't help but ask myself, *Where an underground chemical-weapons stash was supposed to be?* According to whom? Was this an "eyewitness account" of a defector? Or was this information from one of the exiles? I don't know to this day. At this point, it does not matter

About a month after the *Post* account, *Newsweek* magazine published a similar story about the trials of another site-survey team—Team 5. The article of June 12, 2003, by Adam Piore[5] mentions an Iraqi who told the site-survey team of a "suspected chemical-weapons site" in the desert. The account goes on to say that Team 5 traveled several hours and hundreds of miles in the "sweltering" heat. After taking measurements at the location, team member Lt. Bryan Potts concluded, "There ain't nothing here." He went on to confide in the *Newsweek* reporter, "Before I came over here, I figured for sure they'd probably use [unconventional weapons] … But now I'm really not too sure they had them."[6] I tend to believe if Lt. Potts had been privy to the information I received prior to the Iraq Resolution vote of October 10, 2002, he probably would have been "not too sure they had them" then as well.

The beginning of the end of the hunt for a WMD program in Iraq took place on January 28. 2004. I recall it quite clearly. I happened to be on the road and had spent the night of the 28th in a hotel. As a perk, the hotel provided copies of *USA Today* to each room. When I opened the door to my hotel room the morning of January 29, 2004, I observed a copy of the newspaper with a photograph of weapons inspector David Kay staring back up at me. On the front page, Kay's photo was accompanied by the headline, "We were almost all wrong."[7] The article by John Diamond covered Kay's remarks delivered at a briefing for the Senate Armed Services Committee the day before. The weapons inspector went on to say, "and I certainly include myself here."[8] Although I don't usually say, "I told you so," I have definitely not shared in the mea culpa extravaganza that has been so prevalent since Mr. Kay's testimony. In fact, at the time, I thought to myself as I read the story that Mr. Kay would have been more accurate to say, "Almost all of us were wrong."

After David Kay's testimony before the Senate panel, there were still many in the Bush administration, specifically, and Republicans, generally, who found it necessary to excuse the commander in chief from the task of uncovering the WMD. So they continued to suggest Saddam had excused his WMD program from Iraq. The claim was made that Iraq's WMD had been carried away for safekeeping in a foreign country, namely, Syria. I often heard this explanation of why the U.S. military with its effective control over the entire country of Iraq could not locate evidence of the justification for our country's initiation of violence on a foreign people. I was continually amazed by the inane rationale behind such an assertion. The basis for the removal of WMD from Iraq by Saddam Hussein was characterized by a chronology of events that went something like this:

1. Saddam Hussein has weapons of mass destruction.
2. The world should know this because he expelled the weapons inspectors from Iraq.
3. Saddam has used these horrific weapons against his own people, obviously to preserve his regime.
4. The U.S. military has invaded Iraq.
5. The invasion is for the purpose of "regime change."
6. "Regime change" will not be defined by a kind of time-out for the Hussein regime, meaning the United States is not going to allow Saddam to sit in a corner of Iraq and think about how bad he has been so that after his time-out, he may return to get along with others.
7. Actually, everyone knew what "regime change" meant before the invasion, and that was exactly what happened after that incident in which the world observed Saddam Hussein gazing up from a hole in the ground as all of those soldiers aimed automatic weapons at his face.

8. And to reiterate, "regime change" included Saddam attached to that rope that was too short to allow the weight of his body to be supported by his legs—which is what legs are for—and, thus, it had to be supported by his neck—which is not what the neck is for.

9. And so knowing all of this about what "regime change" had in store for him, Saddam, in a fit of uncharacteristic and irrational altruism, ordered the removal of the one possible instrument that could have been used against the invading superpower and given that oncoming military behemoth reason for pause in its mission to end his reign of terror.

10. Finally, according to the same scenario, Saddam would have his vengeance from the grave when the WMD that he could have used to defend himself was ultimately supplied by Syria's governing regime to some terrorist group and used against the United States.

11. After which time, the United States would have invaded Syria for the purpose of "regime change," found the leader of Syria in a hole in the ground, performed the same weight-bearing experiment at the end of a rope with *him* just after *he* ordered the removal of the one unconventional-weapon system that would have given a reason for pause to the last remaining superpower who was coming to help *him* keep *his* appointment with the hangman that sent *him* to the grave so *he* would have his vengeance, etc.

As logical as all that sounds, there would be no discovery of nomadic WMD. According to the findings of the Iraq Survey Group as reported by Dana Priest in the *Washington Post* on April 26, 2005, "Iraqi officials whom the group was able to interview 'uniformly denied any knowledge of residual WMD that could have been secreted to Syria.'"[9] Additionally, according to the Post coverage of the group's final report, "Although Syria helped Iraq evade U.N.-imposed sanctions by shipping military and other products across its borders, the investigators 'found no senior policy, program, or intelligence officials who admitted any direct knowledge of such movement of WMD.'"[10] With what we know of Saddam Hussein, if he was willing to use these terrible instruments of war on his own people, why would he not have used them against the invaders? As we learned earlier, U.S. service personnel such as WMD site-survey team member Lt. Bryan Potts believed Saddam would defend his regime to the end with these devastating weapons.[11] Saddam likely knew his fate as early as the first night of the invasion in March 2003. It was unlikely he thought he would be less dead if he withheld the use of his WMD and sent them to Syria.

CHAPTER 11

THE TRUTH EMERGES

AS the hunt for the evidence of a program of WMD progressed toward its fruitless end, I began to ask the same questions that everyone else was asking. Once again, I did not vote against the Iraq Resolution because I knew, definitively, there was no WMD program in Iraq. I did so because the intelligence was not sufficient to justify initiating a military conflict. But I was still almost hopeful that I would be proved wrong. The consequences of the United States invading a foreign country that was no imminent threat would be profound. All my questioning ultimately led me to one simple inquiry, "Who was responsible for proffering the notion that Saddam constituted such an imminent threat to the United States?" It was at this time I began to learn more about the personnel and the activity of a small group of advisors in the Pentagon. Let me share this information with you.

Shortly after the terrorist attacks of 9/11, an organization was created in the Pentagon to assist the secretary of defense's office in its assessment of intelligence gathered by the United States government. The Office of Special Plans (OSP) was under the direction of Undersecretary of Defense for Policy Douglas (Doug) Feith. The existence of this small unit was known to me before the invasion of Iraq. Originally, I understood it to be more of a consultative body to aid the secretary in the assimilation and analysis of the various intelligence streams available to him. It was not until after the distressing news of the lack of WMD evidence that I learned members of the OSP had played a much more critical role in the intelligence "analysis" before the votes in the Congress.

The OSP was responsible for much of the analysis of intelligence used by the Bush administration to make its case that Saddam Hussein's WMD

program constituted an imminent threat to the United States. But how
could this group of very smart people see the same intelligence members of
Congress were considering and conclude such a program existed? If I had
problems with the intelligence, I thought these "analysts" in the Pentagon
would be much more skeptical. There had to be something else. There had to
be a motivation that was at work with which I was unfamiliar. But what could
it be? The answer would not be long in coming.

As the number-three man at the Department of Defense and the individual
under whose direction the OSP operated, Doug Feith was the obvious choice
for my initial attention. He had extensive government experience, having
worked in the Reagan administration. Upon leaving the Pentagon in 1986,
Feith established a law firm with partner Marc Zell, who was a resident of
Israel.[1] Feith was an outspoken advocate for the security of Israel and, in
1996, participated in a discussion that resulted in a policy proposal entitled
"A Clean Break: A New Strategy for Securing the Realm" (hereafter referred
to as "Clean Break"). Published by the Institute for Advanced Strategic and
Political Studies, the paper was a thesis for the economic and physical security
of Israel.[2]

I came across "Clean Break" in the early days of my research of Mr. Feith.
In surfing the Web, I was struck by the frequent allusions to "Clean Break"
in reports of the undersecretary of policy at the Pentagon. As a student of
the Bible and a member of the United States House of Representatives, I was
initially intrigued by the use of the term "realm" in the paper's title. Generally,
citizens of and advocates for Israel do not often refer to the modern state as
a realm. Rather than describing the Jewish state in such Davidic terms, today
it is generally considered a democracy. To hearken back to a time when Israel
was governed by a divinely appointed king informed me that this individual,
Doug Feith, considered the land of his forefathers to be similarly divinely
appointed for a chosen people. "Clean Break" actually alluded to this idea
when the participants in the discussion spoke of a homeland for Jews and
described "our claim to the land—to which we have clung for hope for 2000
years."[3] This type of passion for a native homeland expressed by a naturalized
citizen of the United States was not unusual. However, this was an interesting
perspective from Mr. Feith, who was born in the United States and confirmed
by the Senate to serve in a high-level position in the Department of Defense.
While the paper was widely circulated, its primary purpose in 1996 was to

benefit the incoming government of Israel led by newly elected Prime Minister Benjamin Netanyahu. There was that name again.

As I stated earlier, a colleague of mine had mentioned Mr. Netanyahu's name in a relevant conversation shortly before the vote in the House. The conversation concerned a rather impassioned presentation by Mr. Netanyahu to members of the House prior to the vote on the Iraq Resolution. The speech concerned the threat posed by Iraq. My colleague informed me the former prime minister's address so motivated him to action that the House member felt as though he could lead troops into battle against Saddam Hussein. There seemed to be more of a nexus between "Clean Break" and Mr. Netanyahu's presentation to House members in 2002 than I could presume was coincidental. At this point, I need to remind the reader that I was not present at this particular appearance of Mr. Netanyahu's but am proceeding based on my colleague's comments.

As motivational as Mr. Netanyahu was concerning the threat of Iraq in 2002, Feith and his co-authors suggested to the newly elected prime minister in 1996 that he should "forge a new basis for relations with the United States—stressing ... strategic cooperation on areas of mutual concern." The discussion paper also recommended an "effort [that would] focus on removing Saddam Hussein from power...—an important Israeli strategic objective...." At this point, I thought there was no way that Feith, his fellow discussers, or Prime Minister Benjamin Netanyahu could have imagined a more beneficial environment in which a "focus on removing Saddam Hussein from power" could have led to any better "strategic cooperation on [an area] of mutual concern"[4] with the United States. It was, after all, the case that the father of the commander in chief had been the target of an assassination attempt by that same Saddam Hussein.

While the list of co-discussers of "Clean Break" included the likes of well-known former U.S. government employee Richard Perle, Feith's first boss in the Reagan administration, it was another name that was of more interest in my research. That name was David Wurmser. Mr. Wurmser was, at the time, employed by the Department of Defense. His assignment was in the OSP, and his boss was Doug Feith. Wurmser was working for Feith, who was working for Deputy Secretary of Defense Paul Wolfowitz.

Approximately two years after participating in the "Clean Break" discussion, Feith cosigned an "Open Letter to the President." The letter is included in a Web-based "compendium of documents from official and private sources"[5] known as "Iraq Watch." Iraq Watch is a product of the Wisconsin Project on Nuclear Arms Control affiliated with the University of Wisconsin. In the letter, Feith and thirty-nine of his colleagues recommended to then president Bill Clinton "a comprehensive *political and military strategy* for bringing down Saddam [Hussein] and his regime"[6] (emphasis added). Joining Feith as signatories were Paul Wolfowitz and David Wurmser.

In both instances—the "Clean Break" discussion and the "Open Letter" to President Clinton—all three players—Wolfowitz, Feith, and Wurmser—were employed in positions outside of the government. At the time of the publication of the "Open Letter" in 1998, Wolfowitz was dean of the John Hopkins University School of Advanced International Studies; Feith was managing attorney for the law firm of Feith & Zell; and Wurmser was director of the Middle East program at the American Enterprise Institute. Opinions held by the three were well known before George W. Bush took office in January 2001.

I have observed in my years of political experience an interesting thing about opinions held by private citizens. These opinions—especially passionately held *published* ones—tend to find their way into public policy when those same private citizens transition to government service. For Douglas Feith's and David Wurmser's published viewpoint on deposing Saddam Hussein to find its way into U.S. foreign policy following September 11, 2001, would not only be convenient, it would have precedent. After all, if the beliefs articulated in John Quincy Adams's speech material at a Fourth of July celebration in 1821 can find their way into The Monroe Doctrine—the most famous foreign-policy pronouncement in the history of the republic—in 1823, why couldn't a similar fate have been realized in 2001 by the sentiments expressed by the discussers of "Clean Break" in 1996 and the writers of the 1998 "Open Letter" to President Clinton? It was at this point that I began entertaining the notion that the various links were something more than coincidental.

In determining the motivation of key players in the marketing of intelligence suggesting the presence of a WMD program in Iraq, I received further insight in the form of a March 30, 2004, article in a Capitol Hill newspaper, *The Hill*. Remembering that intelligence analysis many times requires one to recognize patterns, the *Hill* report helped to construct a mosaic. This mosaic was made up of a coalition of the willing that had blossomed vis-à-vis the Iraq conflict.

I had concluded that I was right in my belief that the intelligence did not support the allegation of a WMD program in Iraq. The search for evidence to support that allegation had ended in failure. Having drawn that conclusion, I saw more evidence of the true justification for our military presence in Iraq as I read the *Hill* article one afternoon during a short break that day from House proceedings.

In his article, entitled "Jewish Defections Irk Dems," Alexander Bolton begins by observing, "Senate Democrats are seeking to counter defections by … Jewish donors to the Republicans."[7] The "defections," according to the article, are the result of a "growing allegiance between the GOP and leaders in the Jewish community."[8]

Bolton points out that George W. Bush got less than 20 percent of the backing of Jewish voters in his first campaign for president. Two years later during the midterm congressional elections, the story goes on to say, GOP candidates received almost twice the support from the same community.[9] I can tell you that while there are potentially as many explanations for the significant increase in electoral success of Republican candidates among Jewish voters between the elections of 2000 and 2002 as there are political consultants, there was one fairly prominent vote in both the House of Representatives and the Senate that was cast between November 2000 and November 2002—the vote on the Iraq Resolution in October 2002. Additionally, it was a vote that carried overwhelming Republican support in each chamber. And it is safe to say that Wolfowitz, Feith, and Wurmser played a large part in guaranteeing the success of that vote. So successful, in fact, were these three appointees of the GOP administration that 215 of the 221 Republican members of the House of Representatives who voted on the Iraq Resolution supported it on October 10, 2002, and forty-eight of the forty-nine Republican members of the Senate supported it on October 11, 2002.

Addressing the core issue—fundraising—of the *Hill* article, Bolton explains the GOP received "$100,000 [from the] *president* of the *liberal-leaning* American Jewish Congress," Jack Rosen[10] (emphasis added). Most pundits will tell you that *presidents* of *liberal-leaning* public-policy organizations *do not* contribute to the anti-abortion, anti–gun control, anti–same sex marriage, tax-cutting party of the moral majority. And they most certainly do not do so in the six-figure range. But it is possible that there may have been an issue—and a vote—that was of more concern to the American Jewish Congress than were those domestic issues at the time of Mr. Rosen's contributions. Who can say?

What we can say is that according to research I conducted on the Web site of the Federal Election Commission (FEC), a "Jack Rosen" from New York, NY, employed by "Rosen Partners" contributed $25,000 to the "RNC [Republican National Committee] Republican National State Elections Committee"[11] on October 18, 2002, two days after President George W. Bush signed the Iraq Resolution into law and an additional $25,000 to the same RNC Committee on November 5, 2002, eighteen days after President Bush signed the Iraq Resolution into law. These are the only "soft money" contributions that have ever been made by a "Jack Rosen" and which were, at the time, "exempt from [campaign finance law contribution] limits"[12] according to the FEC Web site.

Finally, Mr. Bolton discloses that Dawn Arnall and her husband, Ronald, who have historically been very generous to the Democrat Party almost exclusively, changed their ways. According to Bolton's article, "Dawn Arnall gave $1 million at *the end of 2002* to the Republican National Committee"[13] (emphasis added). To put this revelation into context, my own examination of FEC records revealed Dawn Arnall contributed $1 million to the "RNC Republican National State Elections Committee."[14] The contribution took place on October 24, 2002. This large contribution was, similar to that of Mr. Rosen's, "exempt from [campaign finance law contribution] limits"[15] and came eight days after GOP President George W. Bush signed into law the Iraq Resolution. Interestingly, my research of FEC records revealed that the seven-figure contribution to Republicans came less than four months after Mrs. Arnall gave $250,000 to the Democratic National Committee.[16] Bolton also reported that at an event "last August" the couple raised $1 million for President Bush.[17] What is important about this newsworthy item is—notwithstanding yet another seven-figure shift in funding suggested—that the article was published in March 2004. The event held "last August" would have taken place in August 2003, three months after President Bush's "Mission Accomplished" speech aboard the USS *Abraham Lincoln*.

As I mentioned earlier, what was of most interest to me in this particular article was the timing that was peculiarly consistent with the various reported defections. I do not mean that they were ideologically consistent but that most of these contributions were consistent with the legislative and bill-signing calendars of late 2002.

While there may have been what was characterized as defections from the Democrat side of the Jewish-American electorate to the George W. Bush camp between his first election and March of 2004, that mosaic of the coalition of the willing was made even richer with a prominent conversion to the Bush camp from the Right. This conversion came from a well-known Republican member of that community during the same time period.

William "Bill" Kristol has a distinguished resumé in public policy, including service as chief of staff for Vice President Dan Quayle in the administration of President George H. W. Bush. He is currently the editor of the *Weekly Standard*—a neoconservative public-policy magazine—and, as such, is a well-known spokesman in the neoconservative political movement.

A thorough examination of neoconservative philosophy would exceed the purpose of this book, and is, therefore, not one that I will attempt. Suffice it to say, however, that neoconservatives believe that the United States can and should use its geopolitical, economic, and military advantages for purposes of propagating democracy abroad. This process would include, if necessary, the removal of despotic regimes. And the geographic region that receives a preponderance of the attention of Bill Kristol and other neoconservatives in this endeavor is, oddly enough, the Middle East.

A series of interviews illustrating the conversion of Mr. Kristol is included in David Aikman's book, *A Man of Faith: The Spiritual Journey of George W. Bush,* published in 2004.[18] While Aikman does not characterize Kristol's experience as anything like a conversion, one can't help but feel that he must have, at least, undergone a significant change of heart.

The relevant portion of the book deals with the response that then candidate for president George W. Bush gave to a question posed by the anchor of Des Moines, Iowa, television station WHO-TV, John Bachman, at a forum on December 13, 1999. The event was held to hear from the Republican Party's six front-runners for the nomination. The question, initially asked of candidate Steve Forbes, was, "What political philosopher … do you most identify with and why?" When the time came for Mr. Bush to answer, he said, "Christ, because [H]e changed my heart."[19] Mr. Aikman spends considerable time in his book recounting the fallout of Mr. Bush's profound proclamation.

Specifically, Mr. Aikman recounts the reaction of Bill Kristol immediately following the forum and his follow-up assessment years later.

Shortly after the "Christ" response at the Des Moines forum by candidate George W. Bush, Bill Kristol appeared on MSNBC and was asked by *Hardball's* Chris Matthews to comment on Bush's answer to Bachman's question. Aikman recounts that Kristol said the "Christ" answer was "'deeply revealing.'"[20] When asked by Matthews to elaborate, Kristol added:

> "It's revealing [of] a kind of narcissism ... I don't deny for a minute the sincerity of it, and I don't deny for a minute the importance of it for Governor Bush. But it is inappropriate, in a way as a matter of public philosophy to appeal to a private religious experience."[21]

Aikman concludes this portion of the account by saying, "Kristol went on to characterize Bush's comment as 'unnerving,' because it was so much about himself. 'In that respect,' he added, 'Bush is like Clinton. It's all—"I feel your pain."'"[22]

Aikman then goes on to observe that change of heart on the part of Kristol I mentioned earlier. It is likely the comments by Kristol were made to Aikman in an interview, given the lack of attribution to some other forum. After detailing the initial Kristol response to Chris Matthews, Aikman writes:

> Interestingly, four years later Kristol seemed to have changed his view from that of the first few days after the debate. "It was politically very skillful," [Kristol] said in the *fall of 2003*. "It totally destroyed the conservative attack on Bush." Kristol, presumably, had in mind the efforts of the other primary contenders, notably Gary Bauer, Alan Keyes, and Steve Forbes, to characterize Bush as wishy-washy on important American conservative moral issues such as abortion[23] (emphasis added).

This was interesting, indeed. And it may have been as Aikman presumes: that Kristol was assessing Mr. Bush's "skillful" foil of attempts by Bauer, Keyes, and Forbes to marginalize the Texas governor's conservative credentials. But wouldn't this have been the assessment of Kristol a "few days after the debate?"[24] With his years of political experience, it's not as if Kristol didn't realize Bauer and Keyes were trying to win the conservative base of the GOP.

The Iowa debate would have been an opportune time for either of the two conservative activists to accomplish this victory. By calling into question the conservative bona fides of the much-better-funded front-runner George W. Bush, Bauer and Keyes would be helping their respective causes considerably. Would Kristol have not seen the genius in Bush's answer at the time? Or was it, as it was with Jack Rosen and the Arnalls, that timing is everything?

I find it interesting that in the fall of 2003, four years after Kristol characterized Bush's "Christ" comments as those of a Clinton-like narcissist, his reconsideration led him to conclude that Bush was, in fact, "politically very skillful."[25] Was there something of some importance to this neoconservative, Bill Kristol, whom Aikman describes to be "of Jewish background,"[26] that took place between December 1999 and the fall of 2003? What could President George W. Bush have done between December 1999 and the fall of 2003 to impress Bill Kristol who, along with Wolfowitz, Feith, and Wurmser, signed the 1998 "Open Letter" to President Bill Clinton, calling for "a … strategy for bringing down Saddam and his regime?"[27] Was there an issue of prominence to the Kristols, Feiths, Wurmsers, and Wolfowitzes on the political Right that would cause them to react to a "Christ" invoker in a politically and chronologically similar fashion as did the "liberal-leaning"[28] Jack Rosen, Dawn Arnall, and Ronald Arnall? I feel I now know the answer to this question.

I recall President George W. Bush's impassioned defense of intelligence supplied by Mr. Feith and Mr. Wurmser that suggested Saddam Hussein maintained a WMD program. So very politically skillful was President Bush in this defense that he convinced not only a large majority of his party's elected officials in Congress with this intelligence but also a comfortable majority of the American populace. President Bush then went on to sign the Iraq Resolution on October 16, 2002, a resolution that led to that historic moment in Baghdad on April 9, 2003, when Saddam Hussein's statue was torn down by U.S. military personnel. All of this culminated just prior to the fall of 2003 in the president's announcement aboard the USS *Abraham Lincoln* that major combat operations in Iraq had concluded. After the USS *Lincoln* speech, the only significant remaining task to be completed in the removal of Saddam Hussein from power would be the actual capture of the tyrant and sponsor of terrorism in the Middle East.

Yes, the Bush administration was concerned, as you will recall, with the possibility that Saddam would supply a weapon of mass destruction to a terrorist organization, given his long ties and support of international terrorism. That support included, as reported by the BBC on March 13, 2003, individual checks of $25,000 and $10,000 to the families of suicide bombers and individuals killed by Israel's military, respectively. The report gave the account of an event where some of these checks were handed out in Gaza at a hall that was decorated with banners proclaiming an alliance between the Palestinian people and the people of Iraq. The banners also disclosed that the funds were supplied by the "hero," Saddam Hussein. Iraq had similarly supplied tens of millions of dollars to Palestinians since late 2000. At this particular event, some of the money was given to the father of a Palestinian killed while operating in a Jewish settlement. What did this bereaved parent think of the Butcher of Baghdad? "Saddam is the only one that has stood with us," the father said.[29] The BBC report made it clear to me why Benjamin Netanyahu, the "Clean Break" discussers, the authors of the 1998 "Open Letter" to President Bill Clinton, and liberal-leaning defectors would consider Saddam Hussein—not Osama Bin Laden—public enemy number one.

What was definite by the fall of 2003 was, like his statue, Saddam would soon not be standing with anyone very much longer. And that would signal an end to a significant financial incentive, such as it is for a suicide bomber, for the furtherance of violence in Israel. This may have been on the mind of some who may have defected or, "interestingly,"[30] converted to the Bush camp, financially, politically, or otherwise.

At this point, some may say, "Ah Hah! Bush sent us to war not because of a threat of weapons of mass destruction but for campaign contributions and possibly even electoral defections from a traditionally Democrat constituency!" In my opinion, nothing could be further from the truth. No doubt, these were beneficial gleanings from a foreign-policy initiative in which well-positioned bureaucrats in the Department of Defense labored to bring about. To say, however, that George W. Bush came into office in January 2001 with the goal of acquiring a larger campaign war chest and more occupants of some electoral big tent is to miss the point when it came to Saddam Hussein. That very point would be made clear by former treasury secretary Paul O'Neill.

CHAPTER 12

A VERY PERSONAL CASE FOR WAR

AROUND the time weapons inspector David Kay delivered the news to the United States Senate that no WMD would be found in Iraq, a book revealing the inner workings of the administration of President George W. Bush was published. In January 2004, Ron Suskind's *The Price of Loyalty: George W. Bush, the White House, and the Education of Paul O'Neill* delivered a glimpse of the president's management style and priorities from the perspective of former Secretary of the Treasury Paul O'Neill.

Early in the book, Suskind describes one of the first official meetings that O'Neill attended with the president. Suskind writes, "On the afternoon of January 30 [2001], ten days after his inauguration as the forty-third president, George W. Bush met with the principals of his National Security Council for the first time."[1] As a member of the president's Cabinet, O'Neill not only had significant input into national economic issues but also played an integral part in national security policy.

After dispensing with an overview of the president's feelings on various topics regarding international relations, Bush called on his national security advisor, Dr. Condoleezza Rice, in "what several observers [at the meeting] understood was a scripted exchange."[2] The president asked, "'So, Condi, what are we going to talk about today? What's on the agenda?'"[3] Dr. Rice's "scripted" response was, "'How Iraq is destabilizing the region, Mr. President.'"[4] Paul O'Neill believed he was witnessing something historic at this first National Security Council (NSC) meeting less than two weeks after President Bush's inauguration. Suskind portrays the historic proceedings this way, "A major shift in U.S. policy [in the Middle East] was under way. After more than thirty years … Now we'd focus on Iraq."[5]

O'Neill summarized the foreign-policy deliberations that took place in the early days of George W. Bush's first term as president, "'From the start, we were building the case against Hussein and looking at how we could take him out … It was all about finding a way to do it. That was the tone of it. The President saying, "Fine. Go find me a way to do this."'"[6]

Shortly before *The Price of Loyalty* was published, correspondent Lesley Stahl of CBS News' *60 Minutes* interviewed Paul O'Neill about the book and his years as George W. Bush's first treasury secretary. O'Neill reiterated to Stahl his impression of the early and overarching national-security priority of the president, son of Saddam Hussein's 1993 assassination target, "'From the very beginning, there was a conviction, that Saddam Hussein was a bad person and that he needed to go.'"[7]

Former treasury secretary Paul O'Neill's perception of President George W. Bush's approach to dealing with Saddam Hussein more than seven months before the terrorist attacks of September 11, 2001, was, "Go find me a way to [remove Saddam Hussein],[8] a bad person … that … needed to go."[9] I tend to believe that it was probably the objective of George W. Bush to find a way to remove Saddam Hussein even before his first NSC meeting, which took place ten days after his first inauguration and more than seven months before the terrorist attacks of 9/11. In fact, I'd put the timing before the inauguration—before election day in November 2000—even before George W. Bush announced in 1999 his intention to run for president. If I were a betting man, I'd put the idea of removing Saddam Hussein from power taking root in the mind of George W. Bush around, say, April 1993.

Not knowing the mind or heart of George W. Bush, I can only speculate as to motive. But with an insider account as vivid as Paul O'Neill's, there is no doubt that George W. Bush definitely possessed a will to bring about the demise of Saddam Hussein. I later learned President Bush's will to go to war with Saddam was tested. That test came during a presentation given to the president by CIA Director George Tenet.

On December 21, 2002, President Bush convened a meeting of his national-security team in the Oval Office. This meeting was covered in a June 20, 2006, PBS *Frontline* documentary entitled "The Dark Side." The documentary was an exposé on the intelligence regarding the global war on terror. "The Dark Side" focused on the efforts to crush al Qaeda after 9/11 as well as the run-up to the invasion of Iraq. Included in the documentary was a host of firsthand accounts to the inner workings of the Bush administration's approach to and usage of the intelligence used to guide its decision making.

One of those firsthand accounts was supplied by Carl W. Ford Jr., director of Department of State Intelligence from 2001 to 2003. He recalled the December 2002 Oval Office briefing that consisted of George Tenet's presentation of the National Intelligence Estimate (NIE) concerning Iraq's alleged WMD program. An NIE is a formal analysis of intelligence of a particular topic of concern to policy makers and political leaders. Mr. Ford said that after President Bush perused the document the CIA director had handed him, the president inquired, "'Is this all we got?'"[10] Mr. Ford then went on to describe his own impression of the president's initial reaction to the intelligence report, saying, "His instincts were right. He saw that there wasn't a lot there. But I guarantee you, that's everything we had. We gave him our best shot, and the president said, '… is that all you got?'"[11]

At this point, the *Frontline* interviewer asked, "And what did [CIA director George] Tenet say?" Mr. Ford immediately responded, "'Slam Dunk.' That was the slam dunk conversation."[12] The prominent reference to the slam-dunk conversation was due to the fact that Director Tenet's use of that particular sports metaphor has become somewhat infamous since it was uttered at the NIE presentation to the president. Infamous in that the reality was that the case for a WMD program in Iraq was much more like an attempted half-court buzzer beater by the home-team captain. You've probably seen one of those before. With time running out, the ball handler heaves the ball in the direction of the goal though he hasn't yet crossed the half-court line. The home crowd—hoping for the best—watches in breathless anticipation as the shot comes up short. And it's not just short. It's not even close.

When I first saw the interview with Mr. Ford, I shared his sense of encouragement. Although it was the middle of 2006 and it had already been determined that there was not a WMD program in Iraq prior to the war, I was relieved that George Bush had seen the same intelligence I had seen and, at least, had questioned it. After I had time to consider what Mr. Ford said in his follow-up, my encouragement melted away.

Following the recounting of the slam-dunk statement by CIA Director Tenet, Mr. Ford mentioned what seemed to be a collective response to that statement. Mr. Ford said:

> Then they said, "Well, if that's true, George [Tenet], if this is right, …
> we're going to have to say it differently. You're going to have to come up
> with different ways of saying this because *a normal person is going to look at
> this and say, 'Is that all you got?'*"[13] (emphasis added)

George W. Bush has always benefited from his folksy manner. Some pundits criticize his perspective as being less than intellectual. Say what you want, that "howdy neighbor" approach has worked for the Texan elected twice governor of the Lone Star State and twice president of the United States of America. If there has been a successful political candidate that has played "a normal person" to win the "normal person"[14] at election time, it's been George W. Bush.

So the quintessential "normal person" candidate turned commander in chief studied the case for the presence of a WMD program in Iraq and concluded, "Is this all we got?" According to a former high-level intelligence official in the federal government who saw the same evidence, a normal person who was not the commander in chief would have studied the case and would have likewise concluded, "Is that all you got?" Why then did the "normal person" commander in chief respond so much differently than a normal person who was not the commander in chief would have responded? This is assuming Mr. Ford was suggesting that a normal person would not have invaded Iraq, given the true nature of the intelligence on WMD, which did not resemble anything like a "slam dunk." This is a question I answered myself with another question. What would a "normal person" do if his father—whom he loved dearly and dutifully—had been threatened with murder by a very unpopular thug? This question was asked under an assumption, as well. And the assumption is the "normal person"[15] son had just been made commander in chief of the most efficient, ferocious, and lethal fighting machine in the world. The question seems to answer itself, doesn't it? But if you are not sure the question answers itself, let me tell you of another question and answer that may be of some assistance.

In July 2007, the Young America's Foundation (YAF) held a conference in Washington, D.C. YAF is a public-policy organization established to introduce and nurture conservative principles among college students. Among the guest speakers at the gathering was syndicated columnist and author Robert Novak. The topic of Robert Novak's presentation was "Campaign 2008" and appeared on C-SPAN's *American Perspectives* television series.[16] A YAF spokesman who had interned with Novak introduced him. The young man described the longtime journalist as "one of Washington, D.C.'s most respected journalists—if not the most respected."[17] The spokesman continued, "Robert Novak prides himself in having *sources in every level of government providing insight into* the inner workings of Congress and *Washington inside politics*"[18] (emphasis added). Novak spoke to the youthful crowd about the status of the conservative movement and the likelihood for electoral success for the GOP in the next presidential election. His talk was not especially heartening.

During Novak's prepared remarks, he summed up the cause of American conservatism's current malaise this way, "What is the problem with the conservative movement right now? Well the obvious problem is we have an unpopular president and an unpopular war."[19] Mr. Novak then reminded his audience that he had been the object of some adverse attention when he opposed the invasion of Iraq. "I caught a lot of criticism. I felt we should not invade Iraq … I was certain there was [sic] no weapons of mass destruction."[20]

After he concluded his opening remarks, Novak opened the floor for questions. After deftly handling a range of issues, including the problems of the Republican Party from a historical context and advice for a conservative who aspires to be a journalist, the columnist was confronted by an attendee from Harvard University who stepped to the microphone. The student asked the following of the conservative journalist who had been in the business for half a century:

> Earlier you said that you were … very confident there were no weapons of mass destruction in Iraq prior to the invasion … I'd like to know who do you think in the government … people high up in decision making positions who shared your view on that and if they did then why did they push forward for the invasion?[21]

Novak, who was accustomed to dealing with the difficult issues in a host of forums, including his stint as a co-host of CNN's always adversarial political talk show *Crossfire*, took on an almost uncomfortable tone. He took a half step back and answered:

> Boy! That is a tough a question because I had sources in the government who showed me documents that indicated to me there was [sic] no weapons of mass destruction … But there were people at a low level in the government who didn't think that there were weapons of mass destruction. Initially Secretary of State [Colin] Powell and Deputy Secretary of State [Richard] Armitage didn't think so but they went along.[22]

Novak alluded to "sources" close to the Iraq issue and in the administration who had furnished him with information. That Robert Novak has access to some of the most sensitive insight into the Bush White House is indisputable. At times, it is this access to sensitive information that has been the story itself, such as, the Valerie Plame/"Scooter" Libby controversy.

Reiterating, Novak said he had sources. Those sources supplied him with information that raised significant doubt regarding the presence of WMD in Iraq. Novak added that there were individuals, to use the description of the questioner, "high up in decision making positions,"[23] who believed, at least, initially, there were no WMD in Iraq. Two of these individuals, according to Novak and his sources, were "Secretary of State [Colin] Powell and Deputy Secretary of State [Richard] Armitage."[24]

Novak then turns to the second part of the young man's question, which was, "Why did they push forward for the invasion?"[25] At this point, Novak paused, looked around the audience, and continued:

> One of the reasons why I would never want to be in government is that necessarily in our system of government the president makes the decisions. *The president really wanted for reasons not entirely based on policy [but] based on personality—he wanted to get rid of Saddam Hussein who had threatened his father*[26] (emphasis added).

Some may say that we cannot read too much into what Novak said here. We should, however, be able to get something out of what "one of Washington, D.C.'s most respected journalists—if not the most respected"[27] conservative journalist was telling his young, conservative compatriots. It is certain that we cannot read into Mr. Novak's reply anything that he did not say. He did not say, "President Bush misjudged the intelligence." He did not say, "Foreign allies were pressuring him to take out Saddam." He did not say, "President Bush believed Saddam was the single greatest threat to stability in the region." He did not say, "President Bush believed Saddam was the single greatest threat to the vital national-security interests of the United States." None of those things can be read into what Robert Novak had learned from his sources. What Robert Novak wanted the next generation of conservative leaders to know about the rationale behind the push for invasion of Iraq was this, "The president ... for reasons ... based on personality ... wanted to get rid of Saddam Hussein *who had threatened his father*"[28] (emphasis added).

It would take a great deal of "spin" to suggest that Novak was saying anything short of this: because it was clear the case for WMD in Iraq was weak—if not completely fabricated—the reason for the U.S. invasion of Iraq was to remove an individual who had conspired to murder the father of the commander in chief. Said differently, the authoritative nature of the response of the highly respected—and connected—journalist to his questioner from Harvard leads us to one conclusion. Sources who supplied Mr. Novak with documents that indicated to him the absence of WMD in Iraq also supplied him with information which indicated the presence of a grudge in the Oval Office.

But as former treasury secretary O'Neill described the president's instructions to the NSC shortly after his first inauguration, he did not as of yet have the "way"[29] to resolve that grudge. That "way" would require information. It would require special information. It would require intelligence. And that intelligence would require the right personnel to formulate it. The right personnel would be found. And the right personnel would find a place in the Pentagon in the Office of Special Plans (OSP).

CHAPTER 13

TOO MANY COINCIDENCES

I mentioned earlier the OSP and the interesting makeup of that creation under the direction of Douglas Feith. Mr. Feith had previously served in the Reagan administration under Richard Perle. In 1996, Perle and Feith contributed to a formal "discussion" which resulted in a publication entitled "A Clean Break: A New Strategy for Securing the Realm."[1] Included in the publication was discussion of the "focus on removing Saddam Hussein from power."[2] Early in the administration of President George W. Bush, Feith returned to the Pentagon as the undersecretary of policy under Deputy Secretary of Defense Paul Wolfowitz. Not long after September 11, 2001, Feith started up the OSP and brought David Wurmser in to head the organization. Wurmser was a fellow discusser on the "Clean Break" material and a cosigner of the "Open Letter to the President" in 1998, as were Wolfowitz and Perle.

If a way was going to be found to rally support for getting rid of a "bad person … that … needed to go,"[3] a pact—or compact—with individuals who had the same opinion of that bad person would be necessary. It would be helpful for the way to remove that bad person to be one bolstered by the intelligence. However, if the intelligence did not support a claim that would provide a way to remove the bad person, it would be equally helpful to have smart people in place who could sell a weak claim.

The claim that Saddam Hussein continued to maintain a WMD program was, indeed, weak. I use the term "weak" diplomatically. Pushing the WMD allegation took substantial effort by smart people. Believe me. You will recall that I was initially puzzled with the idea that smart people in the Pentagon—very smart people in the Pentagon—were looking at the same intelligence I was looking at and they were concluding Saddam was an imminent threat.

I describe the personnel OSP as being very smart because that's what I've heard.

I highly respect the opinions of individuals who are part of our uniformed military. I learned in my twelve years as a member of the House of Representatives Armed Services Committee that America's war fighters are some of the most principled and observant people in the world. An insightful observation was made by Marine Corps General and Chairman of the Joint Chiefs of Staff Pete Pace. In an interview with Jeffrey Goldberg, published May 9, 2005, in the *New Yorker,* General Pace (before he was Chairman Pace) remarked on the intellect of a co-worker in the Pentagon—Undersecretary Doug Feith. General Pace said, "'The less secure an individual is ... the more prone they were to be intimidated by Doug, because he's so smart.'"[4] That opinion of Mr. Feith seemed consistent among leadership in the Department of Defense. Secretary of Defense Donald Rumsfeld described Feith in the same *New Yorker* article as "'one of the brightest people ... I will ever come across.'"[5]

Undersecretary for Defense Policy Douglas Feith wasn't the only very smart civilian in the Pentagon. Deputy Secretary of Defense Paul Wolfowitz, Feith's boss, had recently been dean at a prestigious university prior to his service in the Bush administration. David Wurmser, Feith's subordinate, was a director at a major public-policy think tank before joining the Pentagon to supervise the OSP. These very smart people had seen the same intelligence I had seen. After learning how smart they all were, I concluded that they could not have misjudged the intelligence. I further concluded that they had not misjudged the impact on public opinion of a well-timed yarn about WMD in Iraq controlled by a bad person—as described by former treasury secretary Paul O'Neill.[6]

All of this talk of Wolfowitz, Feith, and Wurmser and their motives for and opportunities in playing key roles supporting the president's initiative to remove Saddam Hussein may sound, as I stated earlier, very coincidental. Add to that the consideration of Jack Rosen, the Arnalls, and Bill Kristol. I was still willing to subscribe to a coincidence theory if not for the information I acquired in my last few months as a member of the House of Representatives.

A conservative Republican colleague from Texas, Rep. Ron Paul, had established an organization named the Liberty Caucus some years before my last year in Congress. The purpose of forming the Liberty Caucus was to

give conservative members a forum to discuss issues from a constitutional
perspective. Congressman Paul would invite various experts to our Liberty
Caucus luncheons in order to enlighten us on a variety of topics relevant to
the legislative calendar.

Initially, many of the conversations focused on free-market economic
principles and principles related to the protection of civil liberties. However,
the discussion turned to a more concentrated effort at discerning the events
surrounding America's foreign-policy predicament in Iraq following the
conclusion that there was not a WMD program that would be uncovered.
Like me, Congressman Paul had voted against the Iraq Resolution.

I need to first point out a couple of things about the Liberty Caucus
luncheons and the discussions about our involvement in Iraq. First, the guest
speakers were not always "conservative" in their political ideology. I say that
not because members knew definitely of a speaker's philosophical inclinations
but because we exercised a sort of "don't ask, don't tell" policy. Congressman
Paul may have had more knowledge than the rest of us on this issue of a
speaker's political ideology. However, it was not something that concerned
the group when it came to the substance of his or her area of expertise. If
I had to guess, I would say that a few of them may have been from the left
end of the political spectrum. But, as I said, that was of little concern to
most of us. What *did* concern us was that each of these special guests had a
unique understanding of some aspect of our foreign policy. Invited speakers
who addressed the Caucus included the former head of the CIA's Bin Laden
unit, Michael Scheuer, and University of Chicago political science professor
Robert A. Pape. Additionally, several had published relevant material that
was of particular interest to either Congressman Paul or another member of
the Caucus. For example, Scheuer's book, *Imperial Hubris,* explained why his
experience at the CIA led him to believe "the West is losing the war on terror,"[7]
and Pape's book, *Dying to Win,* gave an academic approach in describing "the
strategic logic of suicide terrorism."[8]

Upon learning of a prospective speaker, Congressman Paul would make
the necessary arrangements to bring the guest to Capitol Hill for a discussion
with members of the United States House of Representatives. This would
take place if Congressman Paul believed that the prospective guest would, in
fact, bring a beneficial presentation to the group. I point this out not because
Congressman Paul was any sort of control freak. He was just the opposite,

allowing for free flow of dialogue—and, sometimes, monologue from some
of us—at the luncheons. It was, after all, his Caucus, and it was in his office
that we met and ate his food for lunch. Such is the confession of a moocher.

The second thing to point out about these Caucus discussions on Iraq
was that not all of the attending members of the House were of one opinion
on our military involvement in Iraq. While usually only Republican members
of the House attended the Caucus events, membership in the Liberty Caucus
was not restricted to Republican members of the House. Also, relevant to
this issue of "bipartisanship," on many occasions the guest speaker would
leave our Caucus luncheons and deliver the same presentation to a bipartisan
House staff convocation.

As the news began to hit home that we were not going to find a WMD
program in Iraq nor evidence of its being carried away to, say, Syria, some
guest speakers made statements at our luncheons that were difficult for some
attendees—especially members who had voted for the Iraq Resolution—to
hear. That did not stop these House members from coming, however, to the
next potentially unpleasant presentation. I admired them in that, unlike the
picture painted by many pundits and reporters of politicians in general and
members of Congress in particular, these colleagues wanted to know the truth
no matter how difficult it might be to hear.

I found one guest speaker at a Liberty Caucus luncheon, retired Air Force
Lt. Col. Karen Kwiatkowski, PhD, to be particularly interesting. The title of
Dr. Kwiatkowski's presentation was "How Do We Fix the Mess in Iraq?"
Although I learned at the luncheon that Dr. Kwiatkowski was somewhat
prominent in her public disclosures on the fashioning of prewar intelligence
in the Pentagon, I had never heard of her until I got the invitation. I attended
not only to consume the sumptuous fare at Congressman Paul's office but
also to hear from a true "insider." I was planning to ask her questions about
my coincidence theory. The coincidence theory spoke of the prominence of
newsworthy individuals who were—to borrow a description from *A Man of
Faith* author David Aikman—of "Jewish background"[9] and closely associated
with the support of President Bush's success in removing Saddam Hussein
from power. To reiterate, there was the campaign-finance generosity of Mr.
Rosen and the Arnalls as highlighted in the *Hill* newspaper article.[10] There
was the winning over of the neoconservative and *Weekly Standard* editor,
Bill Kristol, mentioned in David Aikman's book.[11] And then, there was the

obvious service of Messrs. Wolfowitz, Feith, and Wurmser in the Department of Defense OSP. I would learn early in her presentation that my question about the coincidence theory would be unnecessary.

After mentioning the standard neoconservative personnel list from the Pentagon with which I was familiar—Wolfowitz, Feith, and Wurmser—Dr. Kwiatkowski mentioned the name of the individual who headed up the OSP in the Pentagon upon the departure of David Wurmser. (Wurmser had moved from the Department of Defense to assume a position in the State Department.) After the terrorist attacks of 9/11, Dr. Kwiatkowski was assigned to the Pentagon's Near East South Asia directorate, which had jurisdiction over Iraq. Dr. Kwiatkowski remarked that Wurmser was succeeded as director of OSP by "Abe" Shulsky. (I later learned his name was Abram Shulsky.) My coincidence theory received a near-fatal blow. Rosen, Arnall, Kristol, Wolfowitz, Feith, Wurmser, and now, Shulsky. To be honest, I do not recall much of the specifics of Dr. Kwiatkowski's presentation after she revealed Mr. Shulsky's name. I was beginning to see through a glass less darkly. The other part of our discussion with Dr. Kwiatkowski that I do remember was her disclosure that she believed she could no longer affiliate herself with the Republican Party. The reason for her departure was that the Republican Party foreign policy had so been given over to neoconservative imperialism and had departed from the founders' warnings against "entangling alliances." This is a refrain that I have heard time and again, in one form or another, from other Republicans—or, rather, former Republicans—as well as conservative independents alike to this day.

Once again, at the mention of Mr. Shulsky's name by the Pentagon insider, retired Air Force Lt. Col. Karen Kwiatkowski, my coincidence theory received a near-fatal blow. The complete demise of my theory occurred at yet another Liberty Caucus luncheon presentation by another distinguished warrior. This distinguished, former war fighter put into words what I had feared was the obvious antithesis to my hope-filled, yet contrived, theory.

CHAPTER 14

CONVINCED

PRIOR to President George W. Bush's ultimate decision to use the authority delegated to him by Congress and the American people to invade Iraq, there were a few former Department of Defense personnel who voiced respectful opposition to such a move. In response to the growing number of such individuals, Rep. Paul contacted a former high-ranking military official who had insight into the workings of the Pentagon at the time of the run-up to the Iraq invasion. The official graciously consented to speak to the Liberty Caucus at one of our luncheons. After speaking to the group, our guest followed the standard procedure for our gatherings and opened the floor for questions. When I contacted the speaker to discuss inclusion of the subject event in this book, I was asked to not attach a name to this account. I am honoring that request.

In response to a question by one of the members, our guest commented on the activity in the Pentagon post–9/11. Being stationed in the Pentagon, he had the opportunity to observe the interaction of the OSP personnel with other military officials. It became clear to him that while the terrorist attacks of 9/11 and the regime of Saddam Hussein were in no way connected, the attacks of 9/11 were, in fact, the open door that the personnel at OSP had hoped for in their desire to topple Saddam.

As the Caucus luncheon progressed, members departed after their questions were answered. This was the custom as members generally had events stacked up. To stay at one engagement longer than necessary meant others would have to be neglected. Near the end of the former official's time with us, only three members remained and I had an opportunity to ask my questions. I then asked, "Were you or anyone else not directly affiliated with the OSP ever in a behind-closed-doors meeting with the personnel of the OSP when they were formulating their intelligence analyses and presentations of such intelligence to civilian or military authorities?"

He responded, "No."[1] He went on to say that not only did he not know of such an attendee to closed-door OSP meetings but that when open presentations were made to Pentagon leadership, OSP personnel would invariably be seated in the room apart from others, usually together against one of the room's walls and away from the conference table where the principle attendees were seated. They would talk among themselves and were, as a group in their work, very exclusive.[2]

This was an important point. Why was the OSP such a closed shop? It could not have been as a result of security clearances. There were literally scores of personnel stationed in the Pentagon with clearances at least as high as those of the OSP personnel. Given that fact, why would personnel assigned to the OSP, an office in the Department of Defense, be so secretive in their deliberations? There had to be a reason for the lack of full disclosure between OSP personnel and other Defense Department personnel. To this day, I do not know why such an exclusive process regarding intelligence existed in the Pentagon. It was especially irrational in light of the fact that this was intelligence that would be used to justify a U.S. invasion of a foreign country.

I then turned to a question on the use of the intelligence that was ultimately made available to the Congress and the country. I had longed to ask this question of someone who was as close to the decision making on this issue as was this particular guest. Yes, I could have asked this question of Secretary of Defense Rumsfeld, of Deputy Secretary Wolfowitz, or even Undersecretary Feith. I'm not sure their answer, however, would have deviated much from the line that had landed us in this unjust fight in the first place. As a sitting GOP member of the House of Representatives, I likewise could have asked Vice President Cheney or even the commander in chief himself. But I was sure that for political purposes as well as purposes of national integrity, they could not have given me any other response than that same line. Given all these reasons, I did not ask any of them. However, I now had the opportunity to ask someone who would answer my question with no consideration of any of those other factors.

My question went something like this, "When one party wishes to convince a second party to engage in an activity that is justified in the view of the first party, it may be that the second party does not believe that the justification for the first party's involvement is sufficient to justify its own. So it is that the first party must find a new justification in order to lure the second party into participating in the same activity. However, it may be that there is not a justification to be found by the first party that would be sufficient to entice the second party into participation. The first party then fashions a justification that is completely fraudulent but is sufficient to entice participation by the second party. It is, therefore, the case that although the second party does become a participant in the activity, the second party is engaged in the activity for the same justification as that held by the first party. That being the case, why did we invade Iraq and why did we engage in 'regime change' in Iraq when we now know that Saddam Hussein did not have a WMD program on September 11, 2001, or thereafter?"

About midway through this rambling preface and subsequent question, the look on our guest's face turned from pained puzzlement to a somewhat uncomfortable grin. He knew where I was going. So I continued so as to not give him anywhere to hide in his answer. "In other words," I asked, "why did Messrs. Wolfowitz, Feith, Wurmser, and Shulsky—"

Our guest interrupted me and interjected, "And Franklin?"[3] While it is terribly bad form for me to interrupt my own literary train of thought and possibly ruin the moment by losing the reader, it is crucial you understand the insightfulness of this interjection. Not only was our guest not hiding, he was going one better on me, literally.

It is important that you understand who "Franklin" is. It is vital, given the congressman asking this very leading question had not previously made the significant connection that would have made the question even more leading.

Not long before this particular guest visited Capitol Hill to talk to members of the Liberty Caucus, Lawrence Franklin was convicted of three felony counts and sentenced to more than twelve years for his part in passing "classified information to an Israeli diplomat and two members of a pro-Israel lobbying group"[4] according to a CBS News report of January 20, 2006. The account concludes by saying, "Franklin at one time worked for the Pentagon's No. 3 official, policy undersecretary Douglas Feith, on issues involving Iran and the Middle East."[5] While I had heard that Franklin was convicted of passing information to individuals concerned with Israel's interests, I did not realize that Franklin had worked for Feith until our guest informed me. Mr.

Franklin was the one individual presumably not of "Jewish background"[6] (to use author David Aikman's description again) brought into the conversation. The addition of his name to the list of actors did not detract in any way from the point I was trying to make in my questioning.

I revised my inquiry and concluded by asking, "Why did Messrs. Wolfowitz, Feith, Wurmser, Shulsky, and Franklin fashion intelligence in support of the spurious claim of the presence of a WMD program in Iraq to draw the United States into a conflict that would lead to the demise of the regime of Saddam Hussein?" With very little hesitation, our guest answered, "In the defense of the nation Israel."[7]

To be fair, our guest could not have said anything else. Given the makeup of the personnel who supplied the intelligence that ultimately sold the Iraq Resolution to Congress and the American people, along with the very public record of those same personnel regarding the regime of Saddam Hussein, any other response would have been just as contrived as that intelligence.

CONCLUSION

WHAT is America to learn from the conflict that we initiated to depose Saddam Hussein? For one thing, the adage that suggests "where there is a will, there is a way" holds true today as it always has. George W. Bush understandably had the will to remove Saddam from power not long after he learned the leader of Iraq had orchestrated the attempted assassination of his father in April 1993. Such is the understanding of well-connected, conservative columnist Robert Novak.[1] And while George W. Bush's ascent to commander in chief of the only superpower military provided a mechanism to exercise that will, he knew that a way to gain political approval would be necessary to actually utilize that military for the desired purpose. Or so claims former secretary of the treasury Paul O'Neill.[2] That way would be fashioned by a group of individuals in the Pentagon who had a lengthy public record of recommendations for action which would lead to the same result—the downfall of Saddam Hussein—albeit, for different reasons.

More specifically, conservatives in America can learn something from this ordeal as well. The immutable principles put forward at our nation's founding are applicable to today. When John Jay observed the history of governments and their operation under men he warned:

> Monarchs will often make war when their nations are to get nothing by it, but for purposes and objects merely personal, such as ... revenge for personal affronts; or private compacts to aggrandize or support ... partizans.[3]

While it is true that President George W. Bush is not technically a monarch, it cannot be argued that the Congress—including scores of Democrats in both the House and the Senate—empowered him to act as such when it handed to him authority to effectively "declare war" on another country, authority exclusively reserved in the Constitution to Congress. It cannot be repeated too often that this empowerment received the blessing of a clear majority of the American people. It is equally important to recall what a staunchly conservative member of the fourth estate, Robert Novak, stated about the president's role in our system of government. When an iconic conservative who has dedicated half a century of his life to reporting on the political class proposes one person must "necessarily ... make the decisions,"[4] you don't get much closer to the monarchy about which Benjamin Franklin warned that lady in Philadelphia.[5]

Additionally, it is clear to many more people today than it was before the congressional votes in October 2002 that Saddam Hussein was contained and posed no significant threat to the security of our republic. After the invasion of Iraq, we soon learned that toppling Saddam gave us no fewer enemies with access to weapons of mass destruction. Hence, in the words of Jay with a second from John Quincy Adams, by attacking Iraq and removing a monster from power abroad, the United States of America would "get nothing by it."[6]

The removal from power and subsequent demise of Saddam Hussein satisfied a "revenge for [a most] personal affront," the attempted murder of the prominent patriarch of a politically powerful family. And it cannot be debated that toppling Saddam was accomplished by means of a "private compact" with political appointees and their underlings in the Pentagon "to support" the ideals of "partizans."[7] In this case, they were partisans operating in a politically bipartisan manner and dedicated to another cause. That other cause was not the salvation of the republic but the securing of the realm.

APPENDIX A

Authorization for Use of Military Force (Enrolled as Agreed to or Passed by Both House and Senate)

—S.J.Res.23—
S.J.Res.23

One Hundred Seventh Congress
of the
United States of America
AT THE FIRST SESSION

Begun and held at the City of Washington on Wednesday,

the third day of January, two thousand and one

Joint Resolution

To authorize the use of United States Armed Forces against those responsible for the recent attacks launched against the United States.

Whereas, on September 11, 2001, acts of treacherous violence were committed against the United States and its citizens; and

Whereas, such acts render it both necessary and appropriate that the United States exercise its rights to self-defense and to protect United States citizens both at home and abroad; and

Whereas, in light of the threat to the national security and foreign policy of the United States posed by these grave acts of violence; and

Whereas, such acts continue to pose an unusual and extraordinary threat to the national security and foreign policy of the United States; and

Whereas, the President has authority under the Constitution to take action to deter and prevent acts of international terrorism against the United States: Now, therefore, be it

Resolved by the Senate and House of Representatives of the United States of America in Congress assembled,

SECTION 1. SHORT TITLE.

This joint resolution may be cited as the "Authorization for Use of Military Force".

SECTION 2. AUTHORIZATION FOR USE OF UNITED STATES ARMED FORCES.

(a) That the President is authorized to use all necessary and appropriate force against those nations, organizations, or persons he determines planned, authorized, committed, or aided the terrorist attacks that occurred on September 11, 2001, or harbored such organizations or persons, in order to prevent any future acts of international terrorism against the United States by such nations, organizations or persons.

(b) War Powers Resolution Requirements-

(1) SPECIFIC STATUTORY AUTHORIZATION.—Consistent with section 8(a)(1) of the War Powers Resolution, the Congress declares that this section is intended to constitute specific statutory authorization within the meaning of section 5(b) of the War Powers Resolution.

(2) APPLICABILITY OF OTHER REQUIREMENTS.—
Nothing in this resolution supercedes any requirement of the
War Powers Resolution.

Speaker of the House of Representatives.

Vice President of the United States and President of the Senate.

Appendix B

Hon. John N. Hostettler of Indiana
Floor Statement

[Page: H7286]

(Mr. HOSTETTLER asked and was given permission to revise and extend his remarks.)

Mr. HOSTETTLER. Mr. Speaker, I thank the gentlewoman from New Mexico for yielding me this time.

Today the question before this body, Mr. Speaker, is not "How shall we respond to the unprovoked attack by a foreign nation upon the United States or its fielded military forces abroad?"

We are not debating "How will we respond to the menace of a political and/or cultural movement that is enveloping nations across the globe and is knocking on the door 90 miles off the coast of Florida?"

Nor, Mr. Speaker, are we discussing a response to an act of aggression by a dictator who has invaded his neighbor and has his sights on 40 percent of the world's oil reserves, an act that could plunge the American economy, so dependent on energy, into a deep spiral.

Finally, Mr. Speaker, and this point must be made very clear, we are not discussing how America should respond to the acts of terrorism on September 11, 2001. That debate and vote was held over a year ago; and our men and women in uniform, led by our Commander-in-Chief and Secretary of Defense, are winning the war on terrorism. It is with their blood, sweat, and tears that they are winning, for [Page: H7287] every one of us who will lay our heads down in peace this night, the right to wake up tomorrow, free.

No, Mr. Speaker, the question before us today is "Will the House of Representatives vote to initiate war on another sovereign nation?"

Article I, Section 8 of the governing document of this Republic, the United States Constitution, gives to Congress the power to provide for the common defense. It follows that Congress's power to declare war must be in keeping with the notion of providing for the common defense.

Today, a novel case is being made that the best defense is a good offense. But is this the power that the Framers of the Constitution meant to pass down to their posterity when they sought to secure for us the blessings of liberty? Did they suggest that mothers and fathers would be required by this august body to give up sons and daughters because of the possibility of future aggression? Mr. Speaker, I humbly submit that they did not.

As I was preparing these remarks, I was reminded of an entry on my desk calendar of April 19. It is an excerpt of the Boston Globe, Bicentennial Edition, March 9, 1975. It reads, "At dawn on this morning, April 19, 1775, some 70 Minutemen were assembled on Lexington's green. All eyes kept returning to where the road from Boston opened onto the green; all ears strained to hear the drums and double-march of the approaching British Grenadiers. Waving to the drummer boy to cease his beat, the Minuteman Captain, John Parker, gave his fateful command: 'Don't fire unless fired upon. But if they want to have a war, let it begin here.'"

"Don't fire unless fired upon." It is a notion that is at least as old as St. Augustine's Just War thesis, and it finds agreement with the Minutemen and Framers of the Constitution.

We should not turn our back today on millennia of wisdom by proposing to send America's beautiful sons and daughters into harm's way for what might be.

We are told that Saddam Hussein might have a nuclear weapon; he might use a weapon of mass destruction against the United States or our interests overseas; or he might give such weapons to al Qaeda or another terrorist organization. But based on the best of our intelligence information, none of these things have happened. The evidence supporting what might be is tenuous, at best.

Accordingly, Mr. Speaker, I must conclude that Iraq indeed poses a threat, but it does not pose an imminent threat that justifies a preemptive military strike at this time.

Voting for this resolution not only would set an ominous precedent for using the administration's parameters to justify war against the remaining partners in the "Axis of Evil," but such a vote for preemption would also set a standard which the rest of the world would seek to hold America to and which the rest of the world could justifiably follow.

War should be waged by necessity, and I do not believe that such necessity is at hand at this time. For these reasons, Mr. Speaker, I urge my colleagues to please vote "no" on the resolution to approve force at this time.

NOTES

INTRODUCTION

1. James Madison, "Federalist No. 41," in *The Federalist Papers of Alexander Hamilton, James Madison, and John Jay,* ed. Garry Wills (New York: Bantam Books, 1982), 204.
2. U.S. Constitution, art. 1, sec. 8, cl. 11 and 14.
3. U.S. Constitution, art. 2, sec. 2, cl. 1.
4. James McHenry, in *Respectfully Quoted: A Dictionary of Quotations Requested from the Congressional Research Service,* ed. Suzy Platt (Washington, D.C.: Library of Congress, 1989), 299.
5. John Jay, "Federalist No. 3," in *The Federalist Papers of Alexander Hamilton, James Madison, and John Jay,* ed. Garry Wills (New York: Bantam Books, 1982), 10.
6. Ibid., 11.
7. John Jay, "Federalist No. 4," in *The Federalist Papers of Alexander Hamilton, James Madison, and John Jay,* ed. Garry Wills (New York: Bantam Books, 1982), 14.
8. Alexander K. McClure, "'Abe' Lincoln's Yarns and Stories," in *Respectfully Quoted: A Dictionary of Quotations Requested from the Congressional Research Service,* ed. Suzy Platt (Washington, D.C.: Library of Congress, 1989), 119.

CHAPTER 1

1. Colin Powell, *My American Journey,* with Joseph E. Persico (New York: Ballantine Books, 1995), 504–10.
2. John Deutch, "Fighting Foreign Terrorism" (speech, Georgetown University, Washington, D.C., September 5, 1996), https://www.cia.gov/news-information/speeches-testimony/1996/dci_speech_090596.html (posted April 3, 2007).
3. Jay, "Federalist No. 4," 14.

4.   Ibid.

5.   Ibid.

CHAPTER 2

1.   Jane Perlez, "Fighting Subsides in Somalia's Capital," *New York Times*,
      January 29, 1991, http://query.nytimes.com/gst/fullpage.html?res= 9
      D0CE0DC1E30F93AA15752C0A967958260.

2.   George H. W. Bush, "Address to the Nation on the Situation in
      Somalia" (speech, Oval Office, Washington, D.C., December
      4, 1992), http://bushlibrary.tamu.edu/research/public_papers.
      php?id=5100&year=1992&month=12.

3.   Mark Bowden, *Black Hawk Down: A Story of Modern War* (New York:
      Penguin Books, 1999).

4.   "Clash of Somali Rivals Leaves 6 Dead, 18 Hurt," *New York Times*,
      August 21, 1995.

5.   Thomas L. Friedman, "Airdrop Proposal Gets Endorsement of
      the U.N. Chief," *New York Times*, February 24, 1993, http://query.
      nytimes.com/gst/fullpage.html?res=9F0CE6D8143BF937A15751C0
      A965958260.

6.   *Sense of House Relating to Deployment of Armed Forces in Bosnia and
      Herzegovina*, HRes 247, 104th Cong., 1st sess., *Congressional Record*
      (October 30, 1995): H 11398.

7.   *Prohibition on Funds for Bosnia Deployment*, HR 2606, 104th Cong., 1st
      sess., *Congressional Record* (November 17, 1995): H 13223.

8.   *Relating to Deployment of U.S. Armed Forces in Bosnia to Enforce Peace
      Agreement*, HRes 302, 104th Cong., 1st sess., *Congressional Record*
      (December 13, 1995): H 14849.

9.   Powell, *My American Journey*, 576–77.

10.   Kent Harris, "As U.S. Forces Leave, Experts Debate Success of Bosnia
      Mission," *Stars and Stripes*, November 28, 2004, European edition,
      http://stripes.com/article.asp?section=104&article=24843&archive=tru
      e.

11.   John Q. Adams, in *Respectfully Quoted: A Dictionary of Quotations Requested
      from the Congressional Research Service*, ed. Suzy Platt (Washington, D.C.:
      Library of Congress, 1989), 120.

12.   James Monroe, "The Monroe Doctrine" (speech, Washington, D.C.,

December 2, 1823), http://usinfo.state.gov/infousa/government/
overview/50.html.

13. Adams, in *Respectfully Quoted*, 120.

14. Monroe, "The Monroe Doctrine."

15. Adams, in *Respectfully Quoted*, 120.

16. Ibid.

17. Monroe, "The Monroe Doctrine."

18. Ibid.

CHAPTER 3

1. George W. Bush, "The Second Gore-Bush Debate," Winston-Salem, NC, October 11, 2000, Commission on Presidential Debates, http://www.debates.org/pages/trans2000b_p.html.

2. George W. Bush, "The First Gore-Bush Debate," Boston, MA, October 3, 2000, Commission on Presidential Debates, http://www.debates.org/pages/trans2000a_p.html.

3. Albert Gore, "The First Gore-Bush Debate," Boston, MA, October 3, 2000, Commission on Presidential Debates, http://www.debates.org/pages/trans2000a_p.html.

4. Bush, "The First Gore-Bush Debate."

5. Albert Gore, "The Second Gore-Bush Debate," Winston-Salem, NC, October 3, 2000, Commission on Presidential Debates, http://www.debates.org/pages/trans2000b_p.html.

6. James Lehrer, "The Second Gore-Bush Debate," Winston-Salem, NC, October 3, 2000, Commission on Presidential Debates, http://www.debates.org/pages/trans2000b_p.html.

7. Bush, "The Second Gore-Bush Debate."

8. Kenneth Allen, "The Third Gore-Bush Debate," St. Louis, MO, October 17, 2000, Commission on Presidential Debates, http://www.debates.org/pages/trans2000c_p.html.

9. George W. Bush, "The Third Gore-Bush Debate," St. Louis, MO, October 17, 2000, Commission on Presidential Debates, http://www.debates.org/pages/trans2000c_p.html.

10. Adams, in *Respectfully Quoted*, 120 (see chap. 2, n. 11).

CHAPTER 4

1. *Authorization for Use of Military Force*, HJRes 64 and SJRes 23, 107th Cong., 1st sess., *Congressional Record* (September 14, 2001): H 5638, S 9443.
2. "Nations Unite to Combat Terrorism," *American Forces Press Service*, February 28, 2002, http://www.defenselink.mil/news/newsarticle. aspx?id=43893.
3. George W. Bush, "President Delivers State of the Union Address" (speech, U.S. Capitol, Washington, D.C., January 29, 2002), http:// www.whitehouse.gov/news/releases/2002/01/20020129-11.html.
4. Ibid (all quotations in this paragraph).
5. Ibid.
6. Ibid.
7. Jim Garamone, "U.S. Responds to Iraqi Aggression, Extends No-Fly," *American Forces Press Service*, September 4, 1996, http://www. defenselink.mil/news/newsarticle.aspx?id=40724.
8. Linda D. Kozaryn, "Patrolling Iraq's Northern Skies," *American Forces Press Service*, June 1, 1998, http://www.defenselink.mil/news/ newsarticle.aspx?id=43185.
9. Phillip T. Reeker, Department of State Press Briefing, July 26, 2001, http://www.state.gov/r/pa/prs/dpb/2001/4295.htm.
10. Ibid.

CHAPTER 5

1. Condoleezza Rice, interview by Wolf Blitzer, CNN, September 8, 2002 (made available on *CNN.com*, January 10, 2003), http://cnn. com/2003/US/01/10/wbr.smoking.gun/.

CHAPTER 6

1. Richard Cheney, "Vice President Speaks at VFW 103rd National Convention" (speech, Nashville, TN, August 26, 2002), http://www. whitehouse.gov/news/releases/2002/08/20020826.html.
2. Richard Cheney, "The Vice President Makes Remarks at the NRCC Gala Salute to Dick Armey and J. C. Watts" (speech, The Washington Hilton and Towers, Washington, D.C., October 2, 2002), http://www. whitehouse.gov/news/releases/2002/10/20021002-15.html.

3. George W. Bush, "Remarks by the President at John Cornyn
    for Senate Reception" (speech, Hyatt Regency, Houston, TX,
    September 26, 2002), http://www.whitehouse.gov/news/
    releases/2002/09/20020926-17.html.

4. Classified briefing. No transcript allowed.

5. Bonnie Azab Powell, "U.N. Weapons Inspector Hans Blix Faults Bush
    Administration for Lack of 'Critical Thinking' in Iraq," *UC Berkeley
    NewsCenter, March* 18, 2004, http://www.berkeley.edu/news/media/
    releases/2004/03/18_blix.shtml.

6. Classified briefing. No transcript allowed.

CHAPTER 7

1. Rice, interview by Blitzer, CNN, September 8, 2002 (see chap. 5, n. 1).

2. *Authorization for Use of Military Force*, HJRes 64 and SJRes 23, 107th
    Cong., 1st sess., *Congressional Record* (September 14, 2001): H 5638, S
    9442.

3. *Authorization for Use of Military Force*, HJRes 64 and SJRes 23, *Cong. Rec.*
    (Sept. 14, 2001): H 5638, S 9443.

4. Jay, "Federalist No. 3," 11 (see introduction, n. 5).

5. Classified briefings. No transcripts allowed.

6. Condoleezza Rice, "Wriston Lecture" (speech, Waldorf Astoria Hotel,
    New York City, October 1, 2002), http://www.whitehouse.gov/news/
    releases/2002/10/20021001-6.html.

7. Cheney, "Vice President Speaks at VFW 103rd National Convention"
    (speech, Nashville, TN, August 26, 2002).

8. George W. Bush, "Remarks by the President at the National
    Republican Senatorial Committee Annual Dinner" (speech, National
    Building Museum, Washington, D.C., September 25, 2002), http://
    www.whitehouse.gov/news/releases/2002/09/20020925-6.html.

9. George W. Bush, "President Bush Outlines Iraqi Threat" (speech,
    Cincinnati Museum Center, Cincinnati, OH, October 7, 2002), http://
    www.whitehouse.gov/news/releases/2002/10/20021007-8.html.

10. Ibid.

11. "On This Day, 1981: Israel Bombs Baghdad Nuclear Reactor,"
    BBCNews.com, http://news.bbc.co.uk/onthisday/hi/dates/stories/
    june/7/newsid_3014000/3014623.stm.

12.   Jay, "Federalist No. 4," 14 (see introduction, n. 7).

CHAPTER 8

1.   "Bush Engages and Persuades Public on Iraq," report from the
      Pew Research Center for the People and the Press, Washington,
      D.C., September 19, 2002, http://people-press.org/reports/display.
      php3?ReportID=161.

2.   Howard Berman, 107th Cong., 2nd sess., *Congressional Record* (October
      8, 2002): H 7286.

3.   Jay, "Federalist No. 3," 11 (see introduction, n. 5).

4.   John N. Hostettler, 107th Cong., 2nd sess., *Congressional Record*
      (October 8, 2002): H 7286–87.

CHAPTER 9

1.   George W. Bush, "President Delivers 'State of the Union'" (speech,
      U.S. Capitol, Washington, D.C., January 28, 2003), http://www.
      whitehouse.gov/news/releases/2003/01/20030128-19.html.

2.   Colin Powell, "U.S. Secretary of State Colin Powell Addresses
      the U.N. Security Council" (presentation, United Nations, New
      York City, February 5, 2003), http://www.whitehouse.gov/news/
      releases/2003/02/20030205-1.html.

3.   Ibid.

4.   Ibid (all quotations in this paragraph).

5.   Classified weekly briefing. No transcript allowed.

6.   Classified weekly briefing. No transcript allowed.

CHAPTER 10

1.   George W. Bush, "President Bush Announces Major Combat
      Operations in Iraq Have Ended" (speech, aboard USS *Abraham Lincoln*
      off coast of San Diego, CA, May 1, 2003), http://www.whitehouse.
      gov/news/releases/2003/05/20030501-15.html.

2.   Barton Gellman, "Odyssey of Frustration," *Washington Post*, May
      18, 2003, http://www.washingtonpost.com/wp-dyn/content/
      article/2006/06/12/AR2006061200918.html.

3.   Ibid.

4.   Ibid.

5.   Adam Piore, "Digging Up the Dirt," *Newsweek* web exclusive, June 12,

2003, http://www.newsweek.com/id/58503.

6. Ibid (all quotations in this paragraph; brackets in the original).

7. John Diamond, "Kay: 'We Were Almost All Wrong,'" *USA Today*, January 29, 2004, A1.

8. Ibid.

9. Dana Priest, "Report Finds No Evidence Syria Hid Iraqi Arms," *Washington Post,* April 26, 2005, http://www.washingtonpost.com/wp-dyn/content/article/2005/04/25/AR2005042501554.html.

10. Ibid.

11. Piore, "Digging Up the Dirt."

CHAPTER 11

1. See the following Web site: http://www.fandz.com/html/zgap2.html#mzell.

2. "A Clean Break: A New Strategy for Securing the Realm," The Institute for Advanced Strategic and Political Studies, 1996, http://www.iasps.org/strat1.htm.

3. Ibid.

4. Ibid (all quotations in this paragraph).

5. See the Web site, http://www.iraqwatch.org/aboutus/index.htm.

6. "Open Letter to the President," various signatories, February 19, 1998, http://iraqwatch.org/perspectives/rumsfeld-openletter.htm.

7. Alexander Bolton, "Jewish Defections Irk Dems," *Hill*, March 30, 2004, 1.

8. Ibid, 7.

9. Ibid.

10. Ibid.

11. See FEC Web site, http://www.fec.gov/.

12. Ibid.

13. Bolton, "Jewish Defections Irk Dems," 7.

14. See FEC Web site, http://www.fec.gov/.

15. Ibid.

16. Ibid.

17. Bolton, "Jewish Defections Irk Dems," 7.

18. David Aikman, *A Man of Faith: The Spiritual Journey of George W. Bush* (Nashville: W Publishing Group, 2004).

19. Ibid., 3.
20. Ibid., 7.
21. Ibid.
22. Ibid.
23. Ibid.
24. Ibid (both quotations in this paragraph).
25. Ibid.
26. Ibid.
27. "Open Letter to the President," February 19, 1998.
28. Bolton, "Jewish Defections Irk Dems," 7.
29. "Palestinians Get Saddam Funds," *BBCNews.com*, March 13, 2003, http://news.bbc.co.uk/2/hi/middle_east/2846365.stm.
30. Aikman, *A Man of Faith*, 7.

CHAPTER 12
1. Ron Suskind, *The Price of Loyalty: George W. Bush, the White House, and the Education of Paul O'Neill* (New York: Simon & Schuster Paperbacks, 2004), 70.
2. Ibid., 72.
3. Ibid.
4. Ibid.
5. Ibid., 74.
6. Ibid., 86.
7. Paul O'Neill, interview by Lesley Stahl, *60 Minutes*, CBS, January 11, 2004, http://cbsnews.com/stories/2004/01/09/60minutes/main592330.shtml.
8. Suskind, *The Price of Loyalty*, 86.
9. O'Neill, interview by Stahl, *60 Minutes,* January 11, 2004.
10. Carl W. Ford Jr., interviewed in "The Dark Side," *Frontline*, PBS, June 20, 2006, http://www.pbs.org/wgbh/pages/frontline/darkside/etc/script.html.
11. Ibid.
12. Ibid (both quotations in this paragraph).
13. Ibid.
14. Ibid (both quotations in this sentence).
15. Ibid (all quotations in this paragraph).

16. Robert Novak, "Campaign 2008" (guest speaker, Young America's Foundation (YAF) National Conservative Student Conf., George Washington Univ., Washington, D.C., July 31, 2007), DVD, originally aired on C-SPAN's *American Perspectives* series.

17. Jason Mattera, "Campaign 2008" (spokesman, Young America's Foundation (YAF) National Conservative Student Conf., George Washington Univ., Washington, D.C., July 31, 2007), DVD, originally aired on C-SPAN's *American Perspectives* series.

18. Ibid.

19. Novak, "Campaign 2008."

20. Ibid.

21. Jack Welch, "Campaign 2008" (attendee, Young America's Foundation (YAF) National Conservative Student Conf., George Washington Univ., Washington, D.C., July 31, 2007), DVD, originally aired on C-SPAN's *American Perspectives* series.

22. Novak, "Campaign 2008."

23. Welch, "Campaign 2008."

24. Novak, "Campaign 2008."

25. Welch, "Campaign 2008."

26. Novak, "Campaign 2008."

27. Mattera, "Campaign 2008."

28. Novak, "Campaign 2008."

29. Suskind, *The Price of Loyalty*, 86.

CHAPTER 13

1. "A Clean Break" (see chap. 11, n. 2).

2. Ibid.

3. O'Neill, interview by Stahl, *60 Minutes*, January 11, 2004 (see chap. 12, n. 7).

4. Jeffrey Goldberg, "A Little Learning," *New Yorker*, May 9, 2005, http://www.newyorker.com/archive/2005/05/09/050509fa_fact.

5. Ibid.

6. O'Neill, interview by Stahl, *60 Minutes*, January 11, 2004.

7. Michael Scheuer, *Imperial Hubris: Why the West is Losing the War on Terror* (Washington, D.C.: Potomac Books, 2004).

8. Robert A. Pape, *Dying to Win: The Strategic Logic of Suicide Terrorism*

(Washington, D.C.: Potomac Books, 2004).

9.   Aikman, *A Man of Faith*, 7 (see chap. 11, n. 18).

10. Bolton, "Jewish Defections Irk Dems," 7 (see chap. 11, n. 7).

11. Aikman, *A Man of Faith*, 7.

CHAPTER 14

1.   Anonymous.

2.   Ibid.

3.   Ibid.

4.   "Man Who Spied for Israel Gets 12 Years," *CBSNews.com*, January 20, 2006, http://www.cbsnews.com/stories/2006/01/20/national/main1224809.shtml?source=search_story.

5.   Ibid.

6.   Aikman, *A Man of Faith*, 7 (see chap. 11, n. 18).

7.   Anonymous.

CONCLUSION

1.   Novak, "Campaign 2008" (see chap. 12, n. 16).

2.   Suskind, *The Price of Loyalty*, 86 (see chap 12, n. 1).

3.   Jay, "Federalist No. 4," 14 (see introduction, n. 7).

4.   Novak, "Campaign 2008."

5.   McHenry, in *Respectfully Quoted*, 299 (see introduction, n. 4).

6.   Jay, "Federalist No. 4," 14.

7.   Ibid (all quotations in this paragraph).

INDEX